St Andrew's Church, Roker

Phaidon Press Ltd
Regent's Wharf
All Saints Street
London N1 9PA

First published 1996

© 1996 Phaidon Press Limited
Photography © 1996 Martin Charles, unless otherwise stated

ISBN 0 7148 3344 4

A CIP catalogue record for this book is available from the British Library.

All rights reserved. No part of this publication may be reproduced, stored in a retrieval system or transmitted, in any form or by any means, electronic, mechanical, photocopying, recording or otherwise, without the prior permission of Phaidon Press Limited.

Printed in Singapore

NA
5471
.R7258
G37
1996

9/25/09 Ray gift

1 Prior's sketch for the decoration of the chancel. The drawing was made in 1927, 20 years after the church had been consecrated.
2 Prior photographed in old age. In earlier years he was remembered as having thick black curly hair and a moustache.
3 Exterior perspective of St Andrew's made by Prior in 1905. Pencil and grey wash.

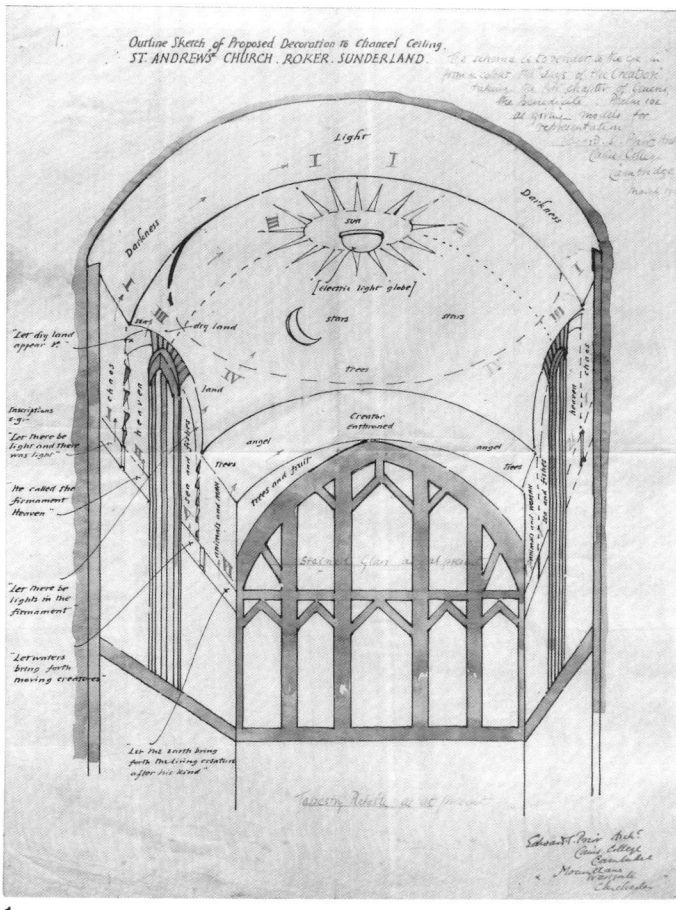

1

In the beginning

'Let there be light and there was light'. Edward Prior took the Biblical myth of Creation, set in motion with these words, for his theme to decorate the chancel of St Andrew's Church, Roker. The sketch he made for this locates quotations from Genesis within a general scheme for depicting heaven and earth as a completed 'garden of delight'. Prior's design was executed in egg tempera by MacDonald Gill (the brother of Eric Gill) who rendered this vision of an Earthly Paradise with a childlike naivety – every tree, every leaf, every fruit, all the fish in the sea, birds of the air, and beasts on the land are painted in single colour with a clear outline.[1]

This is the only decorated surface in the church. Its rich, warm colours and accessible imagery appears in stark contrast to the building itself, which is brutally severe and unrelieved by ornament. It seems almost as if Prior curtailed the Creation story at the point where Adam and Eve walked in the garden in their innocence so that no moral lesson is introduced other than, by inference, the Fall. Its central message is that mankind, driven from Paradise, must 'earn thy bread with the sweat of thy brow'. Redemption through work has been a perennial lesson of the Church. But the meaning of work had taken on a particular significance for architecture during the second half of the nineteenth century following the theories of Ruskin and Morris. They had identified the profound importance of the 'thinking hand' in craftwork and the grave threat posed by industrial production.

The Arts and Crafts movement attempted to implement the precepts of these two men and Prior was instrumental in establishing an Arts and Crafts architecture. Of all movements it is least helpful to think of this one as a 'style'. At the end of a century dominated by style revivalism, Arts and Crafts advocates were united by their conviction that architecture could only become a living art if it disregarded superficial motifs of style and drawn arrangements of revived historical forms. As late as 1901, Prior could remark upon 'an indiscriminate copying of Byzantine, Romanesque, Italian and Indian church models all at the same time ... Surely the pulse of style-worship is failing when its taste knows not what it likes.'[2] All these styles, busily competing as the new century dawned, demonstrated to Prior that any architecture conceived as a style carried no conviction. Arts and Crafts architects believed that a living architecture could only arise by thinking beyond style to the basis in work – materials and techniques.

Arts and Crafts architecture can be either soft or hard – either comforting and familiar, with small-scale spaces and refined detailing, as in the works of Baillie Scott, Gimson or Parker and Unwin, or a sterner architecture, such as Lethaby's and Prior's, responding to the rationalism of the age. Of all Prior's buildings, St Andrew's is the sternest – raw, elemental, uncompromising. Much of his architecture does not bear this stamp, but during his career certain situations seemed to arise that encouraged him to explore a fascination with beginnings or first causes; the original forms, the texture left on materials by the tools. Perhaps Prior's encounter with industrial Sunderland engendered both awe at the sheer power of nineteenth-century engineering mixed with anger at the degenerative appearance of the industrialised world, prompting him to produce, in many ways, his most radical design. Although Pevsner labels St Andrew's 'neo Gothic', closer inspection reveals an almost total absence of any particular stylistic points of reference.[3] It is as if Prior wished to strip away the veils of style

2

to reveal the basis of a building in work; the hard labour of quarrying and cutting stone in particular. In refusing to let any familiar ornamental motifs blunt this recognition, perhaps he hoped that the congregation might grasp, and find support in, the lesson of original man's summons to redemption through work combined with faith.

'A healthy mind in a healthy body'

Edward Schroeder Prior was born on 4 June 1852 in Greenwich, the son of John Venn Prior, a barrister in the Chancery Division. His father died when Edward was 10 years old, and his mother took the the family to Harrow where widows' sons did not have to pay school fees in some circumstances.[4] From Harrow, he went to Gonville and Caius at Cambridge in 1870. He represented his university in the hurdles, long jump and high jump, the last an event in which he became the British amateur champion in 1872. On leaving university in 1874, he became an articled pupil to Richard Norman Shaw. Shaw shot rapidly to eminence in the early 1870s following the success of his 'spectacular perspectives' shown at the Royal Academy exhibitions.[5] In the late 1870s and through the 80s, Shaw brought together many brilliant young architects who were to make their mark, along with Prior, in the Arts and Crafts movement: Ernest Newton, Gerald Horsley, Mervyn Macartney, William Lethaby, Arthur Keen, Sydney Barnsley and Robert Weir Schultz. Pupils were articled for three years before becoming assistants, firstly learning to measure up buildings and then to draw the one-eighth inch scale plans and elevations that formed the basis of practice.

Shaw usually sent his pupils to the Royal Academy schools, and many also attended the Architectural Association Class of Design in the evening but, oddly, Prior registered for neither.[6] Eventually, pupils took responsibility for co-ordinating information on a particular project and Shaw often permitted them to design detail aspects. At the end of his articled period, Prior found himself immersed in actual building as clerk of works to St Margaret's, Ilkley (1877), where he designed some of the fittings.[7] After leaving, Prior continued to work with Shaw on an occasional basis. He made designs for houses in 'a system of concrete construction in which external walls were formed of precast slabs moulded and coloured to simulate brickwork, weather-tiling or half-timber work.'[8] These were produced for a builder often used by Shaw, W H Lascelles, who patented this system of concrete construction illustrated in Shaw's two books of *Sketches for Cottages* published in 1878 and 1882.

Prior's Cambridge background made him rather different from others trained in the office, but Shaw considered him to be 'perhaps the most gifted pupil of them all.'[9] Having learnt from the best possible master, it was perhaps Prior's intellectual nature that gave the peculiar stamp to his own work as an architect, and ultimately led him back to the seat of his learning when he became Slade Professor at Cambridge in 1912. Blomfield, who knew him well, described Prior as combatively argumentative, but always with a twinkle in his eye revealing that it was points of principle and logic he was attacking, not personalities.[10]

Early works

Prior set up on his own in 1880, helped by Shaw's customary gift of a commission or two. The largest, Carr Manor near Leeds, involved extensive remodelling to produce a solid, vernacular-looking stone house dominated by its three-gabled front, possibly influenced by Webb's nearby Rounton Grange.[11] St Peter's Kelsale in Suffolk was a

3

4 Carr Manor, near Leeds. Prior's first commission was a parting gift from Shaw.
5 Middle Road Terrace, Harrow (1887).
6 Harrow School Billiard Room (1889).
7 Harrow School Music Room (1890–91). Prior's perspective drawing reproduced in *The Builder*.

restoration which Prior may already have worked on for Shaw.[12] He took an office at 17 Southampton Street (now Southampton Place) and leased a house at Iver, Buckinghamshire, befitting his status as gentleman-architect. Somewhat curiously, he remained living with his mother at the family home in Harrow, circumstances which were to provide considerable work for his emerging practice. He built The Red House (1883–4) for his eldest brother; St Mary's Mission Hall (1883–4) for the local Temperance Society in which his brother was active; a speculative row of four houses, Middle Road Terrace (1887); Manor Lodge (1883–4); and a series of buildings for his old school – Harrow School Laundry, Laundry Superintendent's House and Workers' Dining Hall (1887–9), funded with a loan from a building society managed by his brother, a Billiard Room (1889) and the School Music Room (1890–91). All red brick buildings, showing the legacy of Shaw's Queen Anne style, these formed part of the architectural mainstream led by George and Peto. Drawing its inspiration from the Low Countries, this period marked a lighthearted interval between the Battle of the Styles and the polemical phase of Arts and Crafts.

Another source of work was his mother's family who lived in and around Bridport, Dorset. The town had lost all its old trades to the railway (even its name had to be changed to 'West Bay' on the GWR's insistence) and Prior's projects formed part of an attempt to relaunch it as a resort – two cousins were on the Board of the West Bay Building Company. His first project for Lodging Houses, Hotel and the Lost Sailor Inn (c1883) was not built, but, much simplified, it became Prior's well-known, craggy Pier Terrace (1884–5). His later, very radical project for the West Bay Club, Bath and Promenade (1894) also remained unbuilt. In between, he had repaired St Mary's, Burton Bradstock (his cousin was vicar), designed with William Lethaby a new south window for St John the Baptist, Symondsbury (1885 – Prior married the vicar's daughter there the same year), and the new Holy Trinity Church, Bothenhampton (1884–9) just one mile from Bridport.[13] Its unusual structure Prior later adapted for St. Andrew's.

His Cambridge connections, and his brother Charles, a Fellow of Trinity, proved to be a further source of work – a series of college alterations, new houses for tutors and Mission Halls for Pembroke College, culminating in the curiously Gothic Henry Martyn Hall (1885–9) and the surprisingly Baroque Cambridge Medical School (1899–1904). It is tempting to see this early body of work as Prior mastering the trade before he found his own radical manner exemplified in The Barn (1896–97), Kelling Place (1903–05) and St Andrew's. But this would be to over-simplify because the last phase of his practice is dominated by quiet, modest houses, such as The Small House, Levant (1909), The Oaks, near Goudhurst, Kent (1910), Windacres, Guildford (1911) and Greystones, Highcliffe, Dorset (1911–13).

In contrast with this little-known body of work, his handful of radical buildings come across as rigorous, logical explorations of intellectual propositions being formulated in the circle of Arts and Crafts architects. Whereas others in the group might keep a tight visual, compositional control over their designs on the drawing board, Prior's intellectual curiosity seems to have driven him to unfold further ideas that generated a project guided not by style but uncompromising logic, an approach that produced buildings that often appear ungainly, even puzzling, but of great originality. The catalyst seems to have been his contact with the ideas of William Morris.

8 Holy Trinity Church, Bothenhampton (1884–9). The bell tower shown in Prior's sketch was not built. The structural system of transverse masonry arches developed here was redeployed for the much larger St Andrew's.

9, 10 Prior's unexecuted, radical designs for a club comprising swimming baths, tea room, shops, library, smoking and reading rooms. One of several designs he made for the West Bay Building Company that was attempting to transform Bridport into a resort.

11, 12 The Henry Martyn Hall (1885–9) and the Cambridge Medical School (1899–1904). Two of a number of projects Prior built in Cambridge where his brother was a Fellow of Trinity College.

8

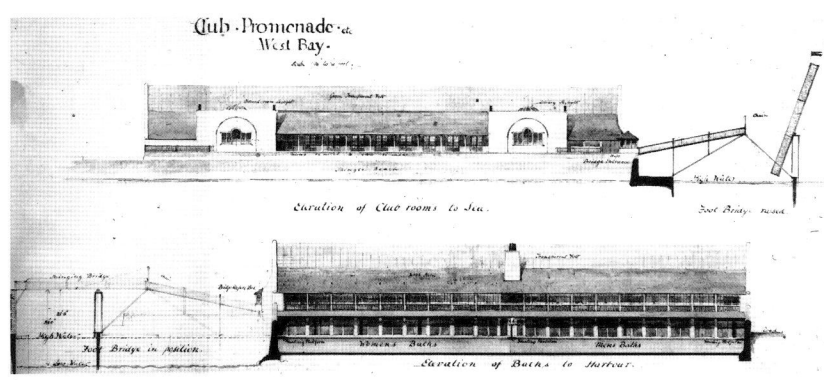
9

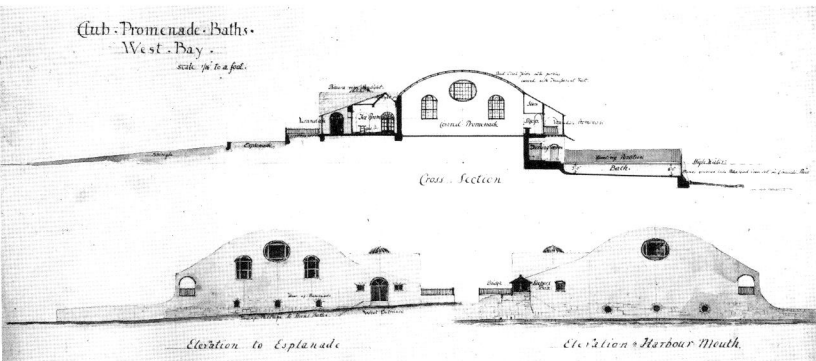
10

11

12

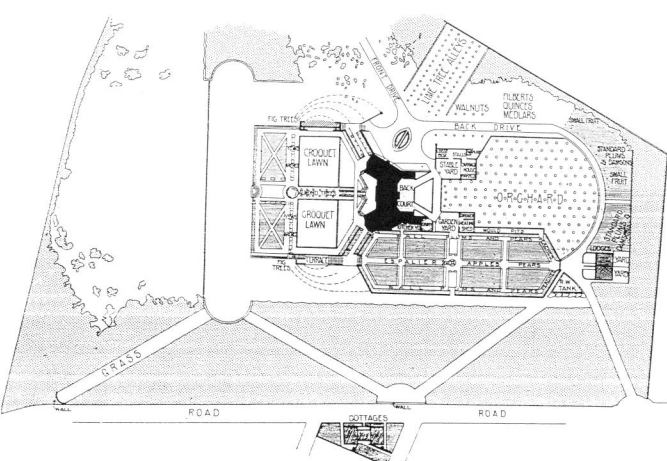

13

14

15

The Art-Workers' Guild

Prior remained close to Shaw's assistants throughout the 1880s and had a significant role in establishing the Art-Workers' Guild, which became the forum for the Arts and Crafts movement. He was on the committee of the St George's Art Society, an informal group drawn almost exclusively from Shaw's office – Newton, Macartney, Horsley, Lethaby and E J May completed the committee – which met regularly in the shadow of Hawksmoor's Bloomsbury church.[14] By 1883, the group had decided that bringing art and architecture together was the key to reviving architecture. Shaw lent support, writing to them that 'If Architecture in England was missing its way it was for the young men to bring her back from professionalism. The Architects of this generation must … knock at the door of Art until they are admitted.'[15]

If we detect a note of equivocation here, it is perhaps because Shaw's work began to take a rather different direction from that of his radical pupils during the 1880s – Shaw towards classicism, the younger men away from codified styles, looking instead to the vernacular for forms resulting from the meeting of materials and workmanship. This issue came to a head in 1884. Robert Kerr, founder of the AA, wrote an article critical of contemporary architecture, calling it an art of 'draughtsmanship, or sketchmanship, regarded as a delightful but delusive sleight of hand, … careless and vague in detail.'[16] Kerr held Shaw responsible for this 'scene painting', a criticism which may have played a part in Shaw turning to classicism for, what Kerr called, 'the nobler qualities' of architecture.

The inspiration for Prior's circle came from William Morris disseminating his ideas on art, handwork and architecture in the 1880s. The decisive moves made by Morris were to disengage Ruskin's linking of handwork with Christian moral sentiments, and to recognize that Ruskin's higher aims for art would require some preliminary groundwork. There is a passage in Ruskin's *Lectures on Art and Architecture* where he acknowledges the need for sound and convenient building as a preliminary to architecture, that could stand as a text for the Arts and Crafts movement:

> It indeed will generally be found that the edifice designed with this masculine reference to utility, will have a charm about it, otherwise unattainable, just as a ship constructed with simple reference to its service against powers of wind and wave, turns out one of the loveliest things that humans produce.[17]

Morris set out to revive the crafts with his own hands as well as words, but just how his example could be extended to architecture became a preoccupation of Shaw's assistants. To explore this they circulated a prospectus, which Prior wrote, inviting artists and architects to join together.

> Architects who feel with us that commercial views have long discredited our Art must desire a return to an association with other Art-workers in a way that existing Architectural societies give no chance of attaining.[18]

From Prior's account we learn that the first meeting in response to this was held on 18 January 1884. An indication of Prior's commitment to Morris's ideals came when he proposed replacing 'Artists and Handicraftsmen' in a motion put by Christopher Day with, '… "Handicraftsmen and Designers in the Arts", and this, seconded by Day, was carried unanimously'.[19] In replacing 'Artist' with 'Designers in the Arts', Prior stresses the doing of things over the broader notion of 'Artist', which could be construed as sensibility more than activity. Prior did much the same in the ensuing discussion on what might be the new Society's name. A succession of names were aired which ended with 'Prior proposing "The Art-Workers' Guild", this was carried.'[20] In formulating this name, stressing work and alluding to traditions of quality control in handicrafts, we see how persuasive Prior was, how he directed Arts and Crafts architecture away from artistic sketchmanship to workmanship, and how deeply he had imbibed Morris's views. This can be explored by examining Prior's first published writing.

'Texture as a Quality of Art and a Condition for Architecture'

A detailed account of this paper given in 1889 at the Edinburgh Art Congress is proposed here, first because it is Prior's first public pronouncement, and secondly, because it is such a little-known, but illuminating, text which helps us better to understand the curious originality of his work that followed. Prior's work tends to be known by comparison and contrast with that of his peers; looking at a single building in detail presents an opportunity to explore his work from within, to see how St Andrew's might be a response to questions raised in his writing.

The National Association for the Advancement of Art in Relation to Industry had been formed in 1888. Its genesis seems to have been bound up with the great success of the first Arts and Crafts Exhibition Society's show that autumn.[21] Morris was President of the National Association and both gave the presidential address – 'The Arts and Crafts of Today' – and chaired the session at which Prior read his paper.[22]

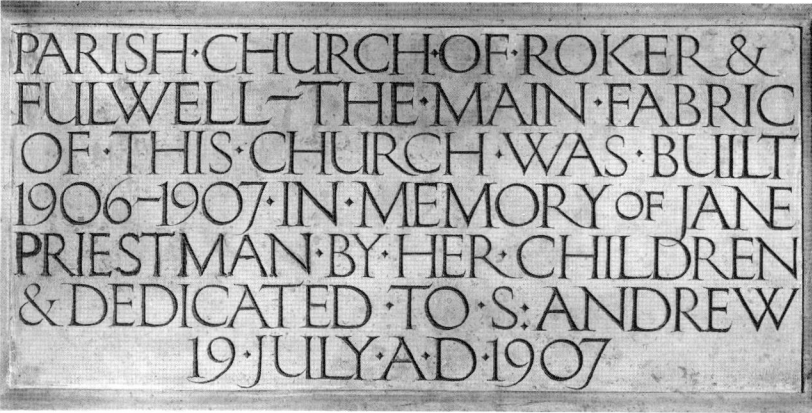

13, 14 Kelling Place (later Home Place), Holt, Norfolk (1903–5), entrance and site plan. Prior in his most radical Arts and Crafts idiom; 'butterfly' plan, concrete walls and floors, most materials obtained by digging a sunken garden.

15 Pier Terrace, West Bay, Bridport, Dorset (1884–5).

16 Memorial tablet in porch at St Andrew's carved by Eric Gill. Gill's promise had been spotted by William Lethaby who diverted him from architecture to lettering during his studies at the Central School of Arts and Crafts.

Prior begins by following Morris in dealing 'not only or chiefly with domes or with palaces, … the Eiffel Tower or Bridge of Forth', but defining architecture as 'common roadside building, village church and shop and cottage, farm sheds and garden walls, pathways set with quickest hedge or sharpened yew. In these familiar things a nation's architecture is shown, the more completely that they are so common and familiar.'[23]

He moves on to criticize contemporary architecture for ignoring texture. Texture, he says, 'has an acknowledged value in painting and sculpture', but is overlooked by architects or unobtainable under the system whereby 'the so-called designer dictates his purpose to the executant'.[24] For Prior, however, texture in architecture means more than 'a condition of material surface':

I would define this quality as that property of surfaces which affects our sense of sight and yet is neither definite form nor definite colour, but would ask you to perceive that what at a nearer, or under a more particular, view is form and decoration, may become at a further distance, or under a comprehensive view, this quality of Texture, but that it does so only when the colour and form have ceased to be recognised as colour or form, when they no longer have the essential effects of these properties.[25]

This is not an easy passage to follow, but its meaning is not unlike that propounded more recently by David Pye in his book *The Nature of Design*; that good design is the manipulation of surface and form to give interest to the eye at every interval from close quarters to distance. Prior seems to be suggesting that architects turn away from historical associations in design and implement instead those qualities found and enjoyed in, for example, a tree – distantly seen as silhouette and form, more closely as structure, detail and surface quality:

There are Nature's own Textures for us to use, or we may borrow from her, and show the grain and figure of her woods, the ordered roughness of her crystallisations in granite or sandstone, or the veinings of her marbles … Then, as evidence of our delight in Texture, we may leave our wood or stone as it comes from the chisel or the saw, to show the fracture that the tool has made, the tokens of its struggle with granite or stubborn oak. So our plaster may show the impress of the loving hand that laid it, our iron will seem to ring under the hammer that shaped it. Then of great value are our jointings of brick and stone, the piercing of our woodwork, the coursing of our slates and tiles. With these we may weave a lace-work over roof and wall and floor. More deliberate are rustications, diapers, and pattern-work, our enrichments, flutings, egg and tongue and dentil courses. These though designed, become merely Texture, when the particularity of their form is obliterated by distance, or fused by the imagination. At a still further distance the larger architectural features themselves – such as windows and piers, pinnacles and buttresses – merge into an undistinguished variegation of surface. Herein lies boundless opportunities for achieving the harmonies of Texture; and so we may provide, that from the first view of even the humblest building, this pleasant Texture should lead on by nearer approach to pleasant detail – itself well textured – and so step by step to the last limits of sight, each step revealing a further veil to be lifted, a further mystery of beauty to be solved.[26]

Prior's conception of texture might be interpreted as his search for a legitimate ground for architecture, enabling him to sidestep the fruitless arguments about appropriate style. While this was a fairly broad aim of Arts and Crafts architects, Prior's trained mind (very few architects at this time went to university) pursued this search a good deal further:

It is a commonplace that art goes to Nature to learn the harmonies of form and colour … Beauty seems to be produced in the universe spontaneously. This is but to say in other words that man, as a part of Nature, must have the faculties to find her agreeable to him; his pulses must beat to the rhythm of her heart, his song must be in the key to her symphonies … Man can have no other source for his ideas of the good.[27]

This idea that Nature is the source of the good and the beautiful was, as Prior acknowledged, a commonplace of late nineteenth-century thought. In his essay entitled 'The Revival of Architecture', Morris had specifically linked the revival with the 'romantic school in literature'.[28] From its beginning in the Lyrical Ballads of Wordsworth and Coleridge, the idea had taken hold that before the Industrial Revolution, ordinary people engaged in everyday lives close to Nature had instinctively produced things of beauty. Wordsworth, for example, sought to revitalise poetry by observing 'the incidents of common life' expressed in 'the real language of men'.[29] Coleridge gave the clearest philosophical expression to this romantic intuition of man's essential bond with nature. He upheld imagination in opposition to the prevailing empirical view of mind which saw thinking as an essentially aggregative act – collecting, sorting, re-combining sense impressions. Defining this as 'fancy', Coleridge believed there also to be an active, originating power at work in the act of thinking, which he called Imagination. This unique

17–19 The Barn, Exmouth, Devon (designed 1896). Prior's first truly radical work; note the broken mass, craggy use of materials, and the combination of logs and concrete for floor construction.
20 Home Place, ground floor plan.
21, 22 Maps from 1898 and 1908 showing the growth of Sunderland north of the River Wear during the time St Andrew's was built. The new church is shown at top centre of the lower map.

17

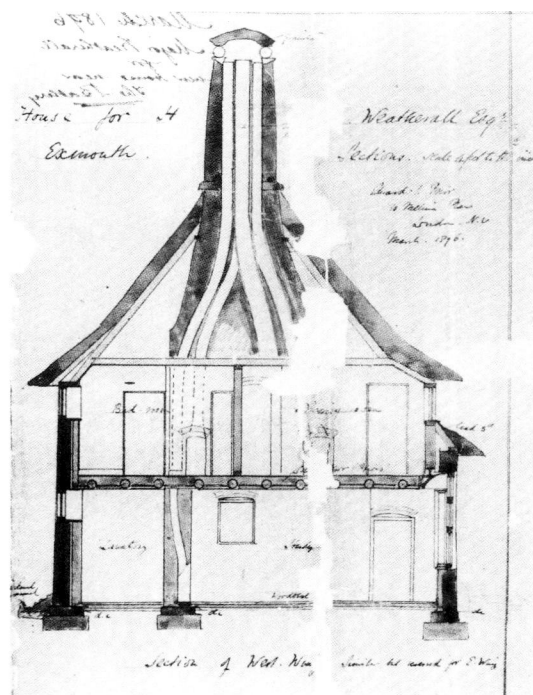

18

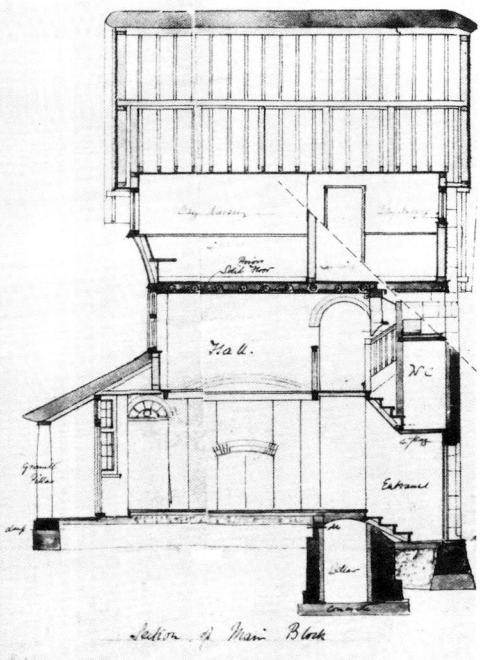

19

attribute of humanity was 'the living Power and prime Agent of all human Perception', he wrote, and 'a repetition in the finite mind of the eternal act of creation'.[30]

It was a short step from Wordsworth's shepherd and cottager to Ruskin's mythical medieval mason. Morris aimed only to bring this down to earth once more, seeing imaginative work in 'thoroughly good, ordinary country buildings, built of the mere country materials, very often of the mere stones out of the fields.'[31] Ruskin's perception of nature was much modified by his evangelism, such that nature appeared to him as God's 'second book' from which the mason could draw inspiration and express faith in his work.[32] Morris's view of nature was secular and more humble, seeing it as the face of the 'homely' earth laboured over by men in sympathy with it, an attitude to things implicit in the crafts. This had become a broad tradition by Prior's time – 'culture' and the 'thinking hand' set up in opposition to utilitarian philosophy and industrial production. Like Morris, he looked to vernacular buildings, but rather than tradition refining detail and form, Prior stressed the raw material presence, the 'beautiful harmonies of Texture, … the rough burnt brick, the rough burnt tile, the handshaped timber and the hand-cast plaster, thatch and tarred boarding, lead lattice, and bubbled glass, traceries of wrought iron, incrustations of moulded lead.'[33] The interesting thing is how elemental Prior's illustrations of texture to be found in Nature are:

The forces of the atmosphere, 'wind and storm, snow and vapour', shape out the solid earth, carving it all into valley and ridge, furrowing each valley with a thousand ravines and every ravine with a thousand chanellings. As the tide passes from the level sands it leaves the expanse ribbed and rippled into the likeness of its multitudinous seas. Every leaf that grows is veined, or blotched, or mottled, every stalk is ribbed, or hairy, or shaggy with scales. Everywhere there is gradation, everywhere dislike of monotony of surface.[34]

Prior not only deepens the investigation into the sympathetic relations between man and nature, but also conjures up a picture of his radical buildings yet to come with their rough, varied and interesting surfaces. Prior hated smoothness; it was unnatural. But, unlike Morris, he saw nature not only as an agent of formation, but also of decay:

… the hand of man, may for a little while plane, smooth or polish [but], untiring Nature goes straight to work 'tamenusque recurret'. The smooth stone or slate is creased and curdled – fretted with lichen, scrolled with moss. The polished metal recovers from the unaccustomed condition as if from some molecular distemper. It crystallises afresh, shows a tarnish, or a still more subtle patina. Here, then, should be our teaching.[35]

We can see Prior, step by step, shifting architecture away from its measure in history or morality towards a condition of geology, away from both historical form and Arts and Crafts refinement through traditions of handwork towards a more rudimentary manner of dealing with material.[36] Some original observations on details continue the thrust of his argument:

Our granite must not be moulded as our metal, nor our marble as our wood. This has been well observed in ancient practice. The most accepted profile of a cornice in stone could almost exactly be reversed to form the profile of a metal standard of the best periods; and it is suggestive to observe that the first follows with curious exactness the contours

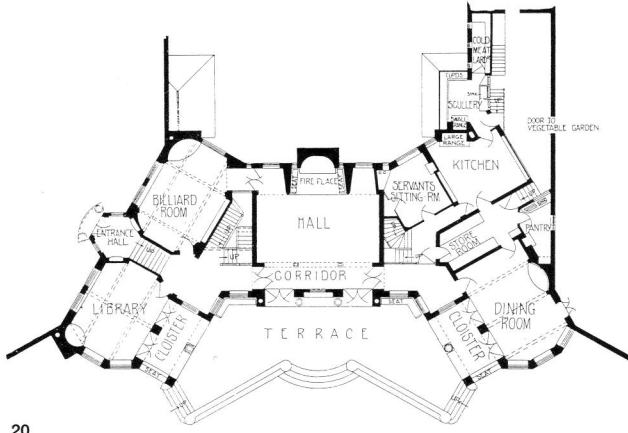

20

of weather-beaten limestone, and the latter almost as accurately the hollows and ridges of rust-eaten iron.[37]

This is the ultimate negation of the predominant idea that architectural ornament is a carrier of historical association. Prior vigorously pursued the fundamental ground of this position beneath time-honoured vernacular traditions reified by Morris to a more-or-less timeless geology where time's mark lies beyond human associations.

Prior concludes his paper by asking rhetorically: 'Will it be said that it was time only that gave these things their preciousness …?'[38] But he rejects this. Reciting a litany of those agents and procedures that had come to intervene between architect and the hand of the workman, he leaves his audience under no doubt that texture was there from the beginning in pre-nineteenth-century buildings and must be incorporated in contemporary design.

Radical works

The first sign of these ideas on texture informing Prior's work came in the model of a house he exhibited at the Royal Academy in 1895. In an article published contemporaneously on 'Architectural Modelling', Prior wrote that, 'architectural drawing has no sense of material, either in colour or texture'.[39] His model was like nothing seen previously. Shaped with his own hands from paraffin wax melted with turpentine, he worked in an extraordinary range of sands, dusts, chalk, coloured powders, even semolina, ground rice and mustard, to give texture.[40] Apparently a great success, the model seems to have led to the commission for The Barn which he designed early in 1896.[41] Intriguingly he was on close terms with Voysey at this time, living next door and both men practising from home. Perhaps Voysey's lauded originality and professional success encouraged Prior to translate his own radical thoughts into design.

The Barn established Prior as an important architect; it was here that he introduced the X-shaped, or 'butterfly' plan. It is often said that Shaw's design for Chesters (1891) was the inspiration for Prior's butterfly plan, and that breaking up the mass represents a picturesque trait in the Arts and Crafts.[42] But the design can be seen to evolve from precepts in Prior's lecture on texture. From the garden-side, its appearance directly expresses the intention to break open the house and let in the sun. This pursuit of first principles in a seaside house, looking directly to the light itself, as a butterfly opens its wings to dry in the sun, seems to offer an explanation of this novel plan.[43] The broken form might also be Prior's determination to allow no specific point of recognition with the rational basis of vernacular construction. In conjunction with the heavy, textured, material presence of the built form itself, it shows how Prior tried to find his own way beyond either historical styles or vernacular logic. The wall surfaces are the very opposite of that 'smoothness' he abhorred; stone quarried locally is left roughly dressed, laid uncoursed and varied with the odd line of large boulders like rocky outcrops or a patch of smaller pebbles from the beach.

With The Barn, Prior used concrete for the first time. The floors were constructed of logs, about 9 inches in diameter, at two and a half feet centres with concrete filling between on timber lathes. Prior used concrete even more extensively in the next house he designed, Kelling Place (now Home Place), near Holt in Norfolk. Designed in 1903, this larger butterfly-plan house pursued, to its logical conclusion, the Arts and Crafts view that architecture should be wholly integrated with the landscape. For here Prior had dug a six-foot-deep sunken garden that provided nearly all the material for the building, 'pebble facings for the walls, and ballast of all kinds for concrete, as well as a good deal of building sand and material for road making and garden paths.' Local stone and Norfolk clay tiles completed the palette for this house whose walls 'were built as concrete masses without planking, and faced with the larger pebbles … The floors were of fine concrete without steel joists, but reinforced with iron chainage'.[44] By the time this innovative, radical, yet deeply-rooted house had been completed, Prior was at work on St Andrew's.

The commission

During the course of the nineteenth century, Sunderland's population grew sixfold to reach 146,000 in 1901; shipping coal and ship-building were responsible. New docks were built, the railway came, and new industries grew up: glassmaking, potteries, ropemaking, ironworks, brewing. Three separate parishes, Bishopwearmouth, Monkwearmouth and Sunderland itself, gradually fused to become one borough. By the turn of the century, only Roker Park survived the spread of houses north of the Wear and St Andrew's Church was built to serve this new community.

Roker stands between Monkwearmouth and the sea. A church had existed at Monkwearmouth since 674 AD when Bishop Benedict Biscop, a Northumberland nobleman and a former Abbot of Canterbury who had studied in Rome, founded the Monastery of St Peter.[45] Only a part of the west porch survives, which now forms the lowest section of the tower; but this was a fortunate circumstance, for Prior was very interested in Saxon architecture and St Peter's was to provide some points of inspiration for him.[46]

21

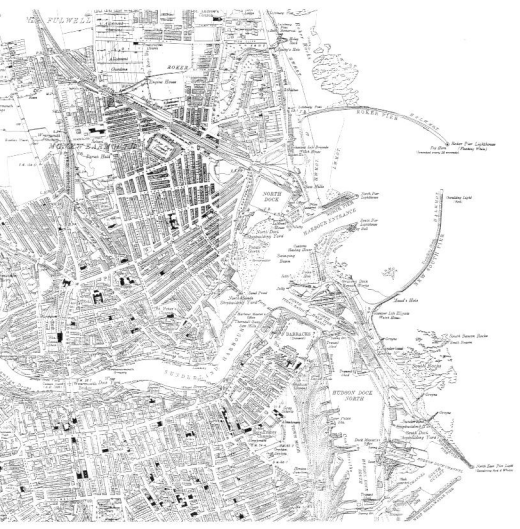

22

12

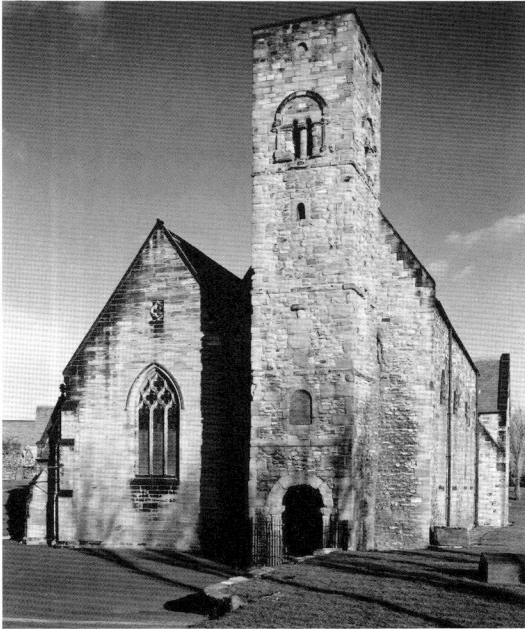

24

23

25

The need for a new church had become pressing by 1903 when the Roker and Fulwell New Church Committee was set up. Public appeals for funds began and applications were made to such bodies as the Free and Open Church Association, the Church Building Society and the Diocesan Building Society in October of that year.[47] At the same time, the Ecclesiastical Commission was approached for permission to divide the parish. This burst of activity had hardly settled when a local ship-builder, a Mr (later Sir) John Priestman, stepped in with an offer of £6,000 towards the construction of the church.[48] With his sisters, he had been looking to make a memorial to his mother (Jane Priestman is commemorated in tablets in the church carved by Eric Gill). Priestman had begun life as a draughtsman, but had risen to have his own ship-building company; he chaired several related companies and was now in a position to impose conditions on his offer, including that the further £3,000 required for the building was to be raised by 30 July 1904; the right to approve the arrangement of the new church; and that he would provide the living for a vicar of his own choice.[49] It seems that Priestman had radical views because the Committee objected to the Reverend Denis Marsh as vicar-designate and requested him 'to nominate some other clergyman – a moderate churchman – as vicar.'[50]

The Bishop of Durham, Bishop Moule, in whose diocese St Andrew's was to be built, was acquainted with Prior for he had been a Trustee of the Henry Martyn Hall.[51] Priestman had been the first man to design an iron steamer in the North-East, so one can imagine that the radically-minded ship-builder would approve of Prior, the experimental builder. We know that Prior was working on the design in 1904, for he submitted an estimate of £9,880 in December of that year.[52]

Prior had preached his radical views to men of the church six years earlier. In an address entitled 'Church building as it is and as it might be', delivered in the Jerusalem Chamber, Westminster, he attacked clergymen who insisted that their architects design in some prescribed 'correct' style. The fight against 'style' had grown throughout the 1890s reaching its climax with Lethaby's call for the term 'architecture' itself to be replaced by 'rational building'.[53] Prior's use of the phrase 'Church building' shows his allegiance to this 'art of building' (as Morris first called it), at a time when the hopes for it were fast disappearing under the emerging Grand Manner, a bombastic baroque revival that followed Queen Victoria's Golden Jubilee. This last flurry of style revivalism marked Edwardian braggadocio about Empire, Commerce and prosperous municipalities. Extravagantly practised by the like of Aston Webb, Belcher, Brydon and Mountfield, it swamped both experimental building and original essays in style. Prior concluded his call for the art of church building by contrasting it with recent practice where 'the professional architect' had been required to provide 'Ecclesiastical style, a method of building which had the form and detail of the great gothic church building which you admired. But taking a professed copy as Art, have you not denied the life of Art?'[54]

Prior's conception for St Andrew's was very straightforward. Three years before the commission, he wrote that the architect's first purpose is to provide 'a dignified distinct building dedicated to the service of the Church … At all times and in all places the greatest architecture has come into existence by the easy plan of building to a purpose.' The clergy should formulate such a programme, he said, then 'the mechanic can proceed to the erection of a simple, and

23, 24 Tower and porch from the Saxon Church of St Peter, Monkwearmouth. Prior's fascination with origins led him to employ the coupled columns from this nearby church in the structure of St Andrew's.

25 Sketch setting out plan for St Andrew's by the young Randall Wells employed by Prior as site architect.

26 Interior perspective made by Prior in 1905. Pencil and sepia washes.

27 Prior's plan of St Andrew's. The lower half shows the wall up to head height, the upper half shows nave window height.

therefore appropriate building – a simply built, and therefore dignified, cathedral.'[55]

Prior had been instructed to seat 600 and to give all the congregation a view of the altar and pulpit. This aim was in keeping with the liturgical movement putting into reverse the changes that had shaped the nineteenth-century church since the passing of the Catholic Emancipation Act of 1829. Between them, Pugin and the Ecclesiologists had curtailed the development of hall-like preaching churches which had begun after the Reformation, Pugin hoping to rekindle medieval faith and charity by returning to gothic architecture, and the Anglican movement combatting the drift to Rome or non-belief in the cities by emphasizing the sacraments and the mysteries of the church as a divine society. This had led to chancel arches, distant altar, fat gothic columns either side of narrow nave, and even the return of the altar screen. As the nineteenth century drew to a close, however, Protestants once again began to play down 'the sacrificial interpretation of the mass and emphasised its communion aspect',[56] stressing the word and breaking down the rigid dichotomy of ordained and lay person.

It is in this liturgical context that St Andrew's needs to be understood. For the striking aspect of the church is the impression made by the vast, open, uncolumned hall. Its direct simplicity affirms Prior's belief that the 'church builder' should be a 'servant' to the aspirations of the clergy, a kind of 'mechanic' to realize liturgical aims to best advantage. Mechanic here is not an inappropriate word, for the church is 52 feet wide, an extraordinary single span for a parish church. With deep, thick arches springing low from massive walls, all the congregation obtain a good view of pulpit and altar. Visibility for the altar is enhanced by the shallow chancel having its walls

26

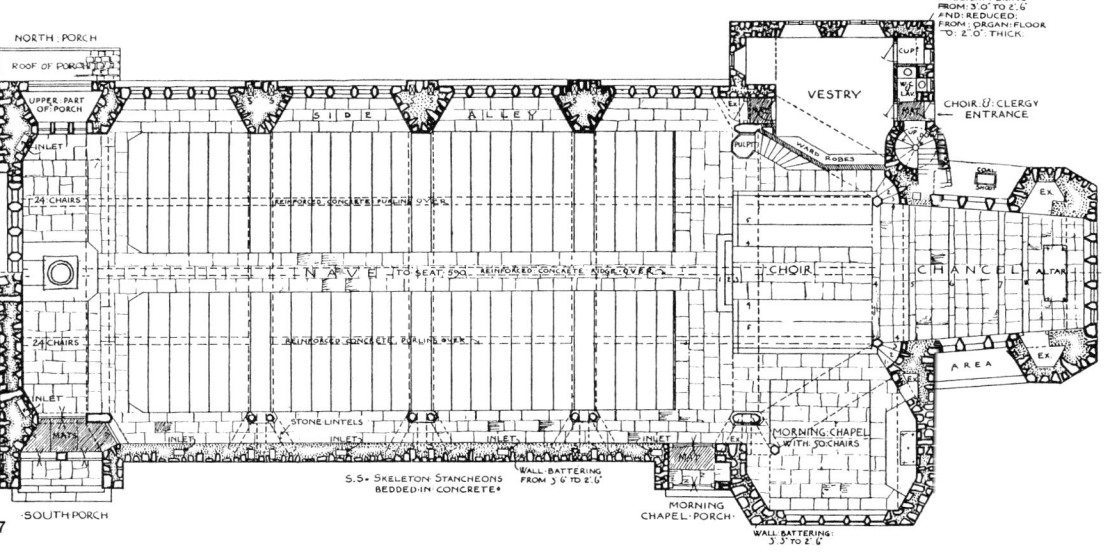

27

28 G F Bodley's St Augustine, Pendlebury (1874), a precedent Prior may have had in mind when cutting a way through internal buttresses.
29 Sketch detail by Randall Wells with comments by Prior. Prior's remarks are on the right and at bottom centre above his initials E S P.
30 Nave wall with entrance porch at intersection with south transept.

28

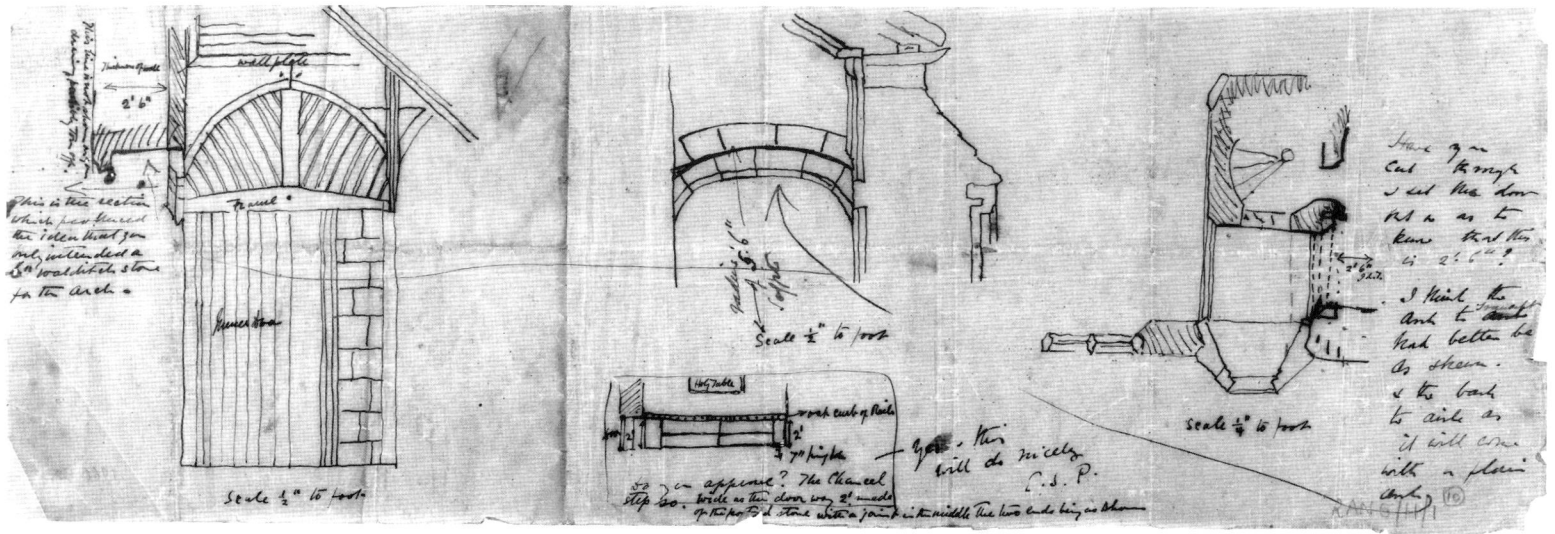

29

tapered in towards the east end. The volume of the nave, with its clear display of structure, has been likened to an upturned boat. While this does appear not unlike a ship at the moment of construction, with its keel and ribs visibly shaping the hull, it would be wrong to pursue this kind of symbolism, although the analogy might be apt for such a ship-building community. Unlike his friend Lethaby, who remained fascinated by symbolism of this kind, Prior seemed to want nothing to come between the direct expression of word and work; he proposed no symbolic structure over and above the work itself. In this he remained close to Morris, seeing in the dignity of labour sufficient and appropriate meaning to embellish the church.

To this end, Prior vigorously pruned his conception of architecture. In his inaugural lecture as Slade Professor delivered five years after St Andrew's was completed, he explained the place of historical styles in his scheme for teaching architecture: 'the teaching of these should be directed to the great creative periods. The actions of building, however complex in their results, have been in themselves few: in a broad sense the wall and the roof comprise them.'[57] Following his lead is perhaps the best way to understand how St Andrew's took shape from its straightforward conception.

The wall

The nave walls are three and a half feet thick at floor level and batter to two and a half feet at window sill height. Piers project five feet into the nave and their inner face is taken up in a shallow arch above each window. The massive buttressing piers, the thickness implied by the closing of the wall above, combine with the low-springing stone arches across the nave to produce the overriding impression of a deeply-protected interior. The uncoursed, random-rubble stone is left unplastered with only the quoins and voussoirs dressed to a flat surface; the thickness of the wall hence finds an echo in the rough, undulating surface of the stone itself.

The stone was quarried from Marsden about three miles north of the site. There was a quarry much closer on Carley Hill, Fulwell, where the same grey magnesium limestone was dug (St Andrew's is sited on the same ridge which ends 200 yards away in 50-foot-high cliffs). But Fulwell Quarry was a huge, mechanized quarry, whereas Marsden 'was worked by quarrymen with their usual tool – the scutcher, a broad bladed pickaxe, which from constant practice they [used] with freedom, yet wonderful precision'.[58] It is an unusual stone found in uneven beds of varying thickness; it does not break naturally along bedding lines but into irregular shapes. Sometimes it is hard and compact, and others it has a curious crystalline structure (in appearance like a tiny version of the Giants Causeway in Ireland) which, when dressed, looks like pumice. Consequently, it is not a stone that lends itself to precisely-rendered detail. Of course, Prior was not interested in delineating a particular style through prescribed detail. No professional purveyor of styles, he pursued his alternative view that an architect should be a mechanic by employing Randall Wells, as site architect. Wells had fulfilled the same role for him at Kelling Place, and before that at All Saints, Brockhampton for Lethaby. There is a sketch plan dated 30 January 1906 showing St Andrew's just pegged out, where Randall Wells signs himself 'resident architect'.[59]

Commencement of the work had been delayed because the Ecclesiastical Commissioners had been slow to authorize the creation of the new parish. In February 1906, the Commissioners had approved Prior's design, although they were concerned about the size of the columns supporting the tower, and also 'the columns under the arches in the nave'.[60] This criticism refers to an ingenious aspect of Prior's design. By bringing the arches down as internal buttresses, he had effectively increased the width between external walls. To maximize width for seating, he pierced through the buttresses to create side passages, transferring the weight to a pair of columns. An important Victorian church where a passage is similarly cut through interior buttresses is G F Bodley's St Augustine, Pendlebury (1874), which Prior would have known. But more interestingly, just such a detail of coupled columns exists at nearby St Peter's as a part of the western porch to the original Saxon church; we can imagine Prior's delight in using it here, providing a constant reminder of the early origins of Christian worship in the parish. Indeed, the plan form itself has Saxon connotations, for Prior argued that the 'ancient oblong chamber' with 'small square-ended sanctuary' represented 'the earliest tradition in our islands'.[61] The simple cushion capitals are like those illustrated in Lethaby's book *The Church of Sancta Sophia*. Lethaby called Romanesque 'the supremely logical building art' that had sprung from the masons' invention of the arch, which in turn encouraged them to generate 'an entirely fresh group of capitals'.[62] These Saxon and Romanesque references show that Prior's search for origins could not rest on empirical practice alone.

Randall Wells did not reply to the Commissioners' concern about the structure until January 1907, by which time the building must have been well advanced. He explained how the tower support had been strengthened by thickening the columns below and building lintels 'corbel fashion with long tails onto the walls.' 'The twin columns in the nave,' he continued, 'have been made 18" diameter and by the method of reinforcement the weight is carried by the wall behind which was thickened to 3' 0" and strengthened with two 18" x 9" skeleton staunchions'.[63] This pair of vertical staunchions 'of light angle iron, cross-braced, 15 ft high … with their ends firmly bedded in the concrete foundations',[64] helps to combat sheer force. A plan showing these suggests that, at one point in the design, the interior of the nave walls was to be left as unfaced concrete. As built, however, the wall is a more conventional construction of stone facings with a core of concrete and rubble. For its first 20 years, the chancel's walls and shallow domed ceiling was left as found when the shuttering was struck. 'They have been left in their rough state,' remarked the Reverend Denis Marsh, 'and the effect, fitting in with the architect's general idea of simplicity and freedom from machine work, is very pleasing.'[65]

A surviving sketch for the vestry entrance by Wells – with notes added by Prior – confirms what we can infer from Wells's letter, and what we know from his work with Lethaby at Brockhampton, of this working relationship between architect, site architect and mason. Prior drew the plans, section and elevations, working out in strategic terms and to some considerable detail the arrangement and appearance of the church. At one level, the building is a straightforward response to the plan serving the liturgical aims of the church; at another level, its appearance results from Prior and Wells seeking out the local stone and seeing what could be done with it. Wells would then not only supervise the work, sorting out problems as they arose, but also engage the masons in decisions about how best to use

30

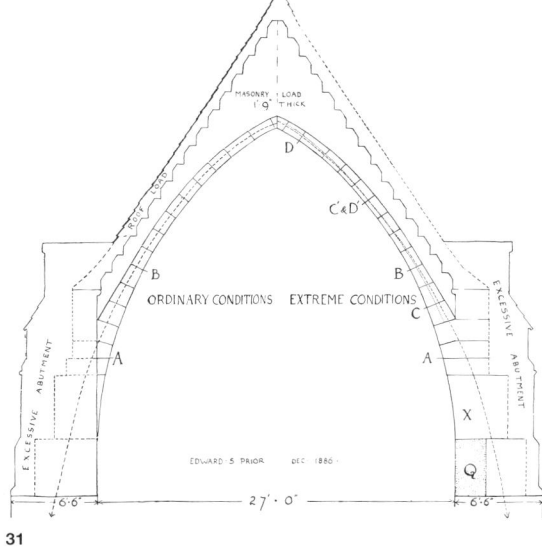

the stone. Jointly promoted by Prior and Lethaby, this experimental, rational, democratic way of building with stone and concrete was inspired by their historical researches into the inventive medieval mason.

The roof

It is hard to imagine now just how radical Prior's structure was. He had first explored this structural system of low-springing arches at Holy Trinity, Bothenhampton because, he said, a timber roof would creak in high winds. Although the span there is only 27 feet 6 inches, low arches springing from unbuttressed walls, having no tie from the roof structure, caused the Incorporated Church Building Society to question its stability and reject the design. There is a furious letter from Prior defending his design's stability mathematically (the maths, he says, had been reviewed by his brother Charles, the Cambridge 3rd Wrangler Lecturer and Professor Burnside, Professor of Mathematics at the Naval College, Greenwich) and by a list of precedents where stone arches formed the principal members of a roof.[66] He demonstrated that such a roof had survived for more than 600 years in the Treasury, Merton College, and that it could span as large as 39 feet 3 inches at The Hall in Mayfield, Sussex. He could also point to his own experience with Shaw, who had used a similar structure spanning 32 feet at Adcote in 1875.[67] At Bothenhampton he remained, like Shaw, otherwise close to traditional construction with pointed stone arches and oak purlins, but at St Andrew's the structure is more radical. Nevertheless, it follows the same principle, as he explained to *The Builder* using a diagram of the structural forces he had prepared for Bothenhampton. Concrete was used, he added, because dressed stone was 'an expensive luxury in the neighbourhood'.[68]

The five massive, transverse, double-radius arches are built of carefully selected larger blocks of the Marsden stone, the quoins alternating between running across the face of the arch and into its depths. The side face of the three-foot-wide arches is the only place where the stone is coursed – following the radius line. Although this suggests that they would be stable if built of solid stone, each is, in fact, reinforced with four iron rods bedded in a concrete core.

The very deep purlins and ridge beam which span 20 feet between supporting arches are also of reinforced concrete, the shuttermarks clearly visible. No detail drawing or specification survives, but a note from Wells says they are reinforced with 'Kahn bars' which were fixed to the bars in the arches.[69] Another possibility they might have considered was to use a steel chain as at Kelling Place. It is worth noting in relation to this that the plan of the church was modified from the first drawings – where the nave walls continued directly eastwards to form the chancel – in that, as built, the corners of the chancel walls were pulled in very close to the inner face of the purlins. Thus, the mass of the chancel walls would help to restrain chains. Furthermore, massive six-foot-wide shallow arches spring obliquely from this junction with the chancel back to the nave walls, giving further restraint. Lateral restraint is similarly provided to the west wall by an equivalent arch and by halving the distance to the first transverse arch. Perhaps options were kept open as construction progressed.

Although concrete remained a very novel form of building construction, Bentley's recently completed concrete domes for Westminster Cathedral had received much publicity, prompting a debate on the role of

31 Prior's sketch section of Holy Trinity, Bothenhampton (1884–9) demonstrating the stability of this structural system which was originally rejected by the Church Building Society. The right hand part of the section shows that the thrusts remain within the structural arches (dotted lines between C C and D D) were the compressive forces to be removed by either wind suction or destruction of the roof by fire.
32 Interior view of Holy Trinity, Bothenhampton.
33 The Hall, Accote, Shropshire (1875) by Richard Norman Shaw. The design and construction of this took place during Prior's time in Shaw's office.
34 Westminster Cathedral (1895–1903), by John Francis Bentley. This view was made before the interior was decorated when the great concrete domes and thick brick walls most impressed radical architects such as Prior and Lethaby whose book on Santa Sophia was much referred to by Bentley in the design.

concrete in architecture. Interestingly, Prior was closely involved in organizing the Seventh International Congress of Architecture which incorporated a session on 'Steel and Reinforced Concrete Construction' where calculations for 'shearing stress', adhesion of concrete to reinforcement, rusting iron, cover to reinforcement, etc, were discussed. This took place at the RIBA on 18 July 1906, when work on the walls of St Andrew's must have been well under way.[70]

The structure was described shortly after completion as 'forming an imperishable skeleton.' However, the way in which the thickness of the walls were developed, its textured surface of stone, and the way that the immense walls were hollowed to capture the play of light from the nave windows, creates an impression more of being inside some vast cellar or cave transfigured by light than a merely rational structural skeleton. The outcome of this, curiously, is an almost exact reversal of gothic architecture. A major impetus of the combined efforts of medieval master mason and monk had been to reduce the appearance of mass to line, hence the invention and elaboration of the rib, clerestory and shaft. At St Andrew's, the presence of the building's mass is emphasized by texture so that mass and light are held in a very different kind of equipoise to a gothic cathedral.[71] In this, Prior brings to a culmination an ambition shared by radical late nineteenth-century architects, to shift the definition of gothic from a historical style to gothic as a way of building. Gothic, in this way of thinking, was seen as quintessentially the art of masonry construction in which invention at the level of structure and detail resulted from a close collaboration between the conceiving mind of the architect and the 'thinking hand' of the mason.

Openings

Prior had spoken of the need to transfer something of the strength of a wall into its openings. At St Andrew's, the blunt directness of this plays a decisive part in shaping the character of the building. The windows in the nave, for example, are subdivided by mullions made of blocks of stone simply feathered away to a thin face. Transomes form cross-bracing (perhaps suggesting the St Andrew's cross), above which a pair of simply canted stones form triangles that help prop the arched opening. On the one hand, this could be seen as Randall Wells pursuing the aim for simplicity from general arrangement to detail in accepting the characteristics of the stone; on the other hand, it might be interpreted in the light of Prior's search for origins.

In his book *Eight Chapters on Medieval Art*, Prior proposed that the only way to understand the particular development of English architecture was to consider 'its special beginnings'. Acknowledging that the Norman Conquest had joined England to the Latin civilizations of Western Europe, he nevertheless contended that 'English culture had already determined its quality in pre-conquest church building, and the Saxon ancestry of our artists, if in the background for a while, asserted itself in some two or three generations.'[72]

In addition to the coupled columns, the small windows in the tower provide the clearest evidence of Prior looking back to Saxon building, for they are direct quotations from St Peter, Barton on Humber, one of the best surviving Saxon churches. With the opening straightforwardly spanned by two stones meeting at the apex (which project from the face to form a hood) these windows are very suggestive of a primitive culture fumbling towards a stone language from a timber precursor.

34

35 St Peter, Barton-on-Humber. A Saxon church showing the 'megalithic' lintelled doorway and 'pilaster' system that Prior refers to in window openings and the tracery at St Andrew's.
36 All Saints, Earl's Barton, another Saxon church known to Prior.
37 All Saint's Swanscombe, Kent (1893–5) by Richard Norman Shaw.
38 St Andrew's tower seen in the context of the Victorian suburb it was built to serve.
39 South elevation drawing by Prior.

35

36

The development of this by Prior into the 'tracery' of the nave also seems to draw inspiration from the 'pilaster' treatment of the same Saxon church tower, or from another well-known Saxon church, All Saints, Earl's Barton. But by transforming the Saxon wall articulation into a tracery window inextricably associated with the gothic desire for light in the walls, Prior stubbornly refuses to allow the design to be stylistically located. More recent scholars have dubbed Saxon architecture 'megalithic' because of its incorporation of large available blocks of stone with rubble, suggestive of what one might expect from the primitive beginnings of a masonry tradition yet to evolve into the refinements of gothic.[73] Prior's nave windows have this attribute much more than Saxon architecture itself. In the chancel, the stone tracery is more elaborate for 'capitals' develop from the mason stepping back a sequence of three stones to a rectangular block. The stones springing from these 'capitals' to support the transome convey a faintly anthropomorphic suggestion of Christ hanging from the cross.

The exterior
'Church architecture, least of all, has been able to go beyond the trivial efforts of traditional picturesqueness; least of all our building has it been monumental.'[74]

Whether or not building simply and massively produces monumentality is a difficult question. But Prior certainly refuses any contrivance that might have made St Andrew's more picturesque. The massiveness of the church is enhanced by setting the nave wall back at window sill level. Probably resulting from careful adjustment of the section to bring light closer to the nave interior, the lower wall is continued upwards as buttresses that find an echo in the curious roofed 'pinnacles' above. While this might be read as a truthful allusion to the structural forces, it is even more an illusion of a stone wall much thicker than it actually is. Porches simply lean against this wall to form entrances; Saxon churches, Prior said, usually had 'no west door, but often porches projecting north and south'.[75] Lack of mediation between the scale of door and building adds to the impression of massive size.

The parapet wall is high and runs round the transepts, giving a long, low appearance to the church. Prior was familiar with those East Anglian churches – Blythburgh, Long Melford, Lavenham – that were built upon the wool trade and sit so well upon the land.[76] The most unusual aspect of St Andrew's, however, is the tower positioned above the chancel. There seem to be several interrelated explanations for this.

Although local legend has it that Prior located the tower nearest to the sea so that sailors could navigate by it, this may have been more metaphorical than literal. The Reverend Denis Marsh described it as 'a beacon for our sailor brothers', and giving 'a parting message of peace and courage, for did not Jesus come walking to the toilers on the sea?'[77] The tower, so positioned, also gives St Andrew's greater visibility from Roker Park Road, the main artery through the suburb.

In addition to these two topographical advantages, Prior seemed to be exploring a formal exercise, and possibly a moral one. From the mid-1870s, Shaw had tried to combine Bodley's new vision of the open single-volumed church with his own of a church with a central tower. A series of projects – St Margaret's, Ilkley, St Michael's, Turnham Green and All Saints, Richards Castle – culminated in All Saints, Swanscome (1893–5) where the long unified volume of nave and chancel pierces through a central tower.[78] At St Andrew's, Prior contrives a vestige of the nave roof line at the east end beyond the tower. The 80-foot-tall, square tower has four hexagonal corner towers containing ventilation shafts and stairs, where the board-marked concrete can be seen. Originally capped with tall pyramid roofs (removed because of wind damage) the corner towers are pulled together with repeated shallow arches above the belfry.

Positioning the tower over the symbolically significant chancel may have appealed on moral grounds. Prior formed the opinion that 'a square-topped, spireless tower' was an expression of 'democratic growth', and had become commonplace because 'bell-ringing was the popular sport. Tower building was in fact an exercise of popular religion itself.'[79] Once the crafts had become secretive and excessively protective in the fourteenth century, Prior believed that the democratic art of building persisted only in the small parish church characterized by its tower and house-like nave.[80] Situated over the crossing, blurring any distinction between nave and chancel, congregation and clergy, bell-ringing is thus given an elevated dignity within the overall meaning of the church here at St Andrew's.

Furnishings and fittings

The east window has stained glass, by A H Payne of Birmingham, depicting the Ascension of Christ. This event, of course, marks a new beginning in Christian doctrine, a great cycle that will end in the Day of Judgment. Below this is a tapestry depicting the visit of the three wise men to the infant Jesus. Made in William Morris's workshop at Merton, this is a copy of a painting by Burne-Jones – an apt choice for the reredos as it brings Morris, his circle and ideals into the focal point of the church. The scene depicted also introduces two images which underscore Prior's pursuit of origins, over and above the central message of Christ's

37

38

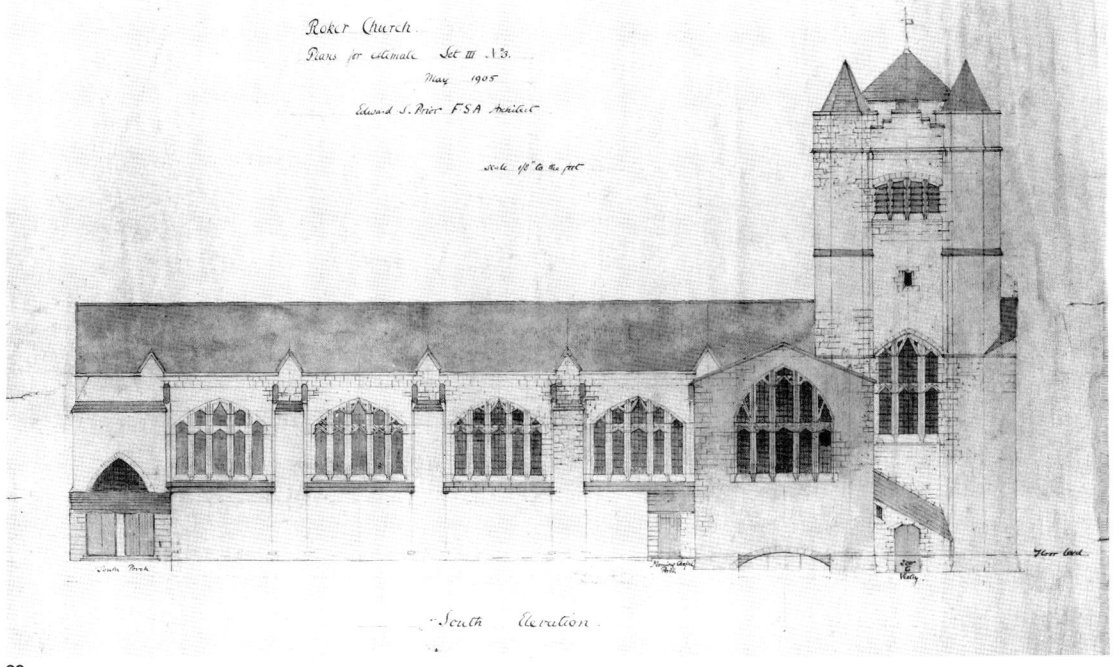
39

40 Back of pews designed by Prior.
41 Detail of window in main entrance door.
42 Working drawing by Prior showing the heating system with plenum beneath chancel and hot air ducts running along the base of nave walls.
43 Detail of carving to font by A Randall Wells.

40

41

earthly birth. The stable is an archetypal primitive hut, like that depicted by Laugier in the eighteenth century when he tried to reformulate a legitimating ground for architecture upon its origins after the collapse of Renaissance cosmology. Furthermore, a wattle fence provides enclosure which carries a suggestion of Semper's nineteenth-century attempt to ground architecture in processes of making – firing, weaving, piling up and jointing. The hearth and woven partition were considered by Semper to be the fundamental archetypes of settlement.[81]

The furniture and panelling in the chancel were made by Ernest Gimson and mark a particularly interesting moment in Gimson's career.[82] Along with Ernest and Sydney Barnsley (who had worked in Shaw's office with Prior), Gimson had taken Morris's call to the crafts most literally, leaving London in 1892 to establish craft workshops in the Cotswolds.[83] At first, their furniture design relied heavily upon techniques learnt from a local joiner, Philip Clissett, but in 1901, Peter van der Waals joined the enterprise. Whether or not by coincidence, from this time on their furniture makes much use of chamfering a technique which originated in the wheelwright's craft where it lightened the weight of the wheel without impairing its strength. Over time, this had come to form decorative treatment of wagons. It was probably adopted for furniture by Gimson because it softened sharp corners and edges, and anticipated wear. At St Andrew's, chamfer upon chamfer produce complex decorative patterns. Prior himself designed the pews which were made by the North of England School Furnishing Company incorporating a similar, if less elaborate, technique.[84] In this way, a reminder of the dignity of work, a reference to time-honoured craft traditions, was brought inescapably close to the congregation.

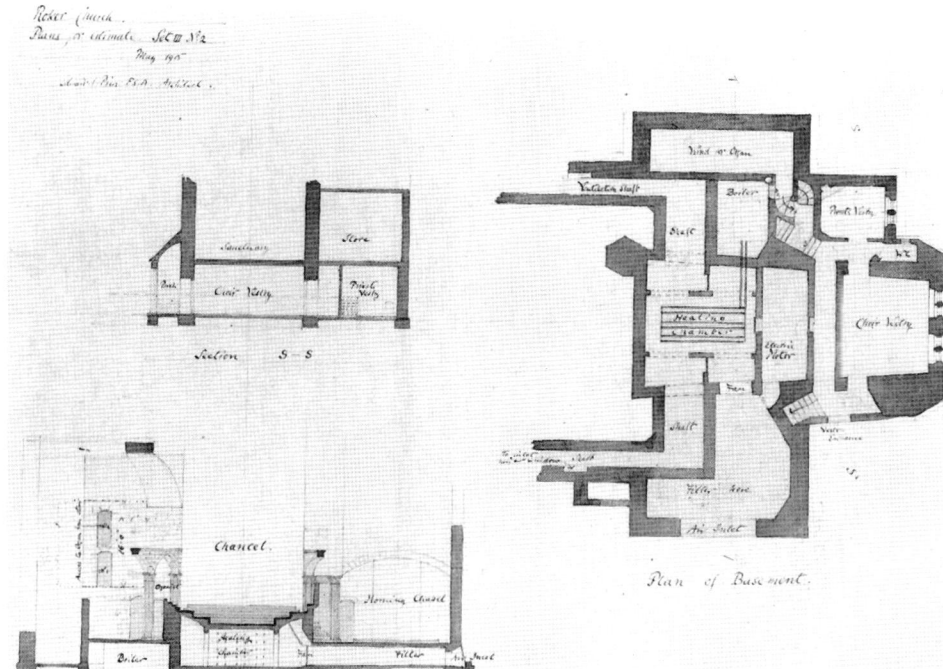

42

43

Gimson also made the ebony lectern inlaid with mother-of-pearl and silver, perhaps a little too elaborate to fit easily into this setting. The cross and the candlesticks on the High Altar were also made at Gimson's Sapperton works by his blacksmith, Alfred Bucknall. These were beaten from wrought iron and lacquered to prevent rusting.

The tall back of Gimson's pews form a screen to the Lady Chapel in the south transept, a dark, stony space, dominated by the glow from Payne's stained-glass window. Taking as its text the words inscribed at the top of the window: 'Come unto me all who are heavy laden and I will give you rest', it is a further celebration of the dignity of labour. Around the central figure depicting the Christ of daily life are representations of all sorts and conditions of men and women, including the mother with her child, the workman with his tools, and a man heavy-burdened whose load is loosened as he looks upon Christ. The organ, paid for and played by Priestman, occupies the other transept.

The clear glass to the nave windows was 'manufactured according to the architect's patent method.'[85] Prior had arranged for a small glassworks, Britten and Gibson of Southwark, to produce 'Prior's Early English Glass', 'a glass with particular qualities'. As the name suggests, Prior developed his specification from a careful study of old work. Produced by blowing the molten glass into a rectangular clay mould, contact with the mould gave it a rough finish. Stretching to reach the corners of the mould, the glass becomes thin and rippled. Prior's specification called for an 'unevenness of thickness ... with or without bubbles and other accidental flaws and irregularities.'[86] This lends a subtle variation to the intensity of light as it plays across the interior. The iron glazing bars were made in Priestman's shipyard.

Electric arc lights in the nave could be 'pulled up into the roof by means of a wire rope and winding apparatus at the side.'[87] The sparkling effect of light reflecting from the irregular face of the glass caused much delight. An inverted 'umbrella'-shaped copper bowl hung in the sanctuary within which a number of electric lamps shone 'onto the white dome, and so [gave] a subdued light to the altar.'[88] The bowl was perforated to give direct illumination to the tapestry. At the centre of the nave, in the space left free for entrance, is an elaborate font carved from Marsden stone by Randall Wells. A striking design, large enough to immerse a child and looking like a cauldron on four corner posts, it is carved with swirling vegetation, perhaps an allusion to early Christian Celtic art prominent in the region.

The walls to the nave are panelled to a height of 7 feet 8 inches in English oak. The boards are of uneven width, fixed with hand-made iron nails. Inset into the wall above are louvred hot-air outlets. Within the mass of the concrete wall, Prior incorporated vertical ducts that connect to a plenum system running beneath the floor to a chamber below the chancel where huge indirect radiators were located. The hot air from these was propelled by 'a Blackman electric fan ... capable of pouring 700,000 cubic feet of air into the church every hour, which means that the air of the church can be completely changed every twenty minutes.'[89] The air intake is beneath the Morning Chapel, the boiler beneath the organ loft.

With all the windows having fixed lights, Prior had to rely largely on the volume of the space and hot air rising to maintain comfortable air conditions for the congregation. However, he did provide two 'doors' in the chancel which are, in fact, 'the lower openings of two ventilating shafts which rise up into the tower.'[90]

44 Inside window to tower showing mass concrete wall construction.
45 Tracery made with pairs of sloping stones that refer to Saxon gabled head window lintels.
46 Elaboration of the gabled heads to form 'proto-capitals' in the chancel.

44

45

46

47 Gabled head lintels over window in tower.

48 View showing how the massive stone arches, supported on paired columns, meet the nave wall with a passage cut through internal buttress to provide side-access to pews.

49 Underside of spiral stair to bell tower.

50 The surface of a piece of Marsden stone showing the curious coarse grain that does not lend itself to fine detailing.

47

48

49

50

51 Detail of pulpit showing Gimson's chamfered joinery resting on a stumpy column of Marsden stone.

51

Rational building or mythical masonry?
With this remark we seem to be on the threshold of modernism; not only do we have a straightforwardly functional plan, a reinforced concrete structure and electric lights, but also an integrated heating and ventilation system. St Andrew's may not have been well known enough for Pevsner to incorporate it into his chain of pioneers leading to what he saw as an inevitable modernism; its 'neo-gothic' appearance would have distracted from the thrust of Pevsner's narrative. But nor could Prior be marginalized later into Pevsner's *The Anti-Rationalists*. He did, however, form one of Goodhart Rendell's collection of late nineteenth-century 'rogue architects', a label just as easily construed as marginalizing those swimming in neither mainstream, forward towards modernism, or backward to historicism. The idea of an 'English Free Style' would have been as disagreeable to Prior as 'smoothness'.

After describing the curious chancel ventilation doors, the Reverend Denis Marsh continued that 'there is a pescina fitted into the wall; that is to say a small basin and water drain, through which the water used at the Holy Communion service is poured away, so that it may return to the earth in a natural way without entering an ordinary drain.'[91] Here we see the gulf that separates our world from Prior's. His conception of the architect as a kind of 'mechanic' of 'rational building' did not presume to enclose all human endeavour within an all-embracing rationality. Prior's vision was largely shaped by that mythical medievalism that ran back through Morris and Ruskin to its roots in romanticism. A central tenet was that man's spirit must resist the triumph of materialism. It insisted upon a symbiotic relationship between man and nature. Prior's conception of 'texture' and the pursuit of the 'thinking hand' – or simply the dignity of hard labour – in the building of St Andrew's represents a last attempt to construct such a world.

Like Lethaby, he came to measure his words on 'rational building', which was all too easily conflated with 'positivism'. Let us not forget that the character of modernism was completely unforseeable when Prior built St Andrew's. But any serious-minded man knew that 'style' was a futile response to the thrust of the age. It was to be another generation before a purely empirical view would prevail and fuse with myths and metaphors of the machine to produce a modernism of many guises that dominated the twentieth century. Now that we recognize this to have been an ideological construction rather than an evolutionary inevitable, explains why we find someone like Prior so interesting. Perhaps, like Morris, whose anger increased as he came to understand the workings of capitalism, Prior saw its imperative here in Sunderland turning small, workshop-like shipyards into industrial sites, and was driven to produce this radical, uncompromising embodiment of his vision whereby labour was dignified and made meaningful.

It is hard for us to recapture this, trapped as we are between uncritical notions of progress and 'traditions' seen to be fogeyish as this style or that. But for Prior, the concept of tradition was more subtle and complex. His pursuit of origins can help us understand how trapped we are, even as we acknowledge how trapped he was by historicism, his search for origins eventually ending up somewhere between Saxon and Norman, Romanesque and Roman. Ever oscillating between an authentic way of working and the first style, it is precisely this impossibility to see things either purely empirically or stylistically that separates Prior's world from ours and makes St Andrew's so intriguing.

Photographs

26 View from the south-west. The raw simplicity of the church, the rough stone, the irregular blocks making the arches, the straight-forward 'megalithic' tracery, are all manifestations of Prior's desire to involve the masons in attaining meaning from the work. Prior went along with Lethaby in arguing for radical building rather than 'architecture'.

28

Detail of wall over south-west entry porch showing the piers projecting above the cornice adding weight to the internal buttresses below. The tracery in the west window and nave windows is both a response to the nature of the stone, its quarrying and working, and also Prior's interest in Saxon masonry. The stone cross bracing might be an allusion to the St Andrew's cross.

Prior contrived a vestige of pitched roof at the east end so that the church appears simply as a single body embracing nave and chancel that pierces the tower. The hooded windows in the stair tower derive from Saxon sources and become elaborated as a motif for the chancel tracery.

Prior believed that a square-topped spireless tower was an expression of 'democratic growth' and had developed as an English tradition because bell-ringing was a popular folk art. He turned to Saxon precedent again in providing no more than a simple lean-to porch on the south nave wall to denote entry.

The cavernous 52-foot-wide nave with its extraordinary single spanning stone arches. Each is, in fact, reinforced with four iron rods beaded in concrete that connect to reinforcing rods in the concrete purlins.

36

Left View into the chancel with its ceiling painted by MacDonald Gill after Prior's design. The chancel walls taper in to create a foreshortening effect that helps bring the altar seemingly closer to the congregation.
Above The organ was donated by John Priestman, principal benefactor to the church, who was also the first organist.
Right Oak panelling in uneven width boards, a detail contribution to help overcome Prior's dislike of smoothness.

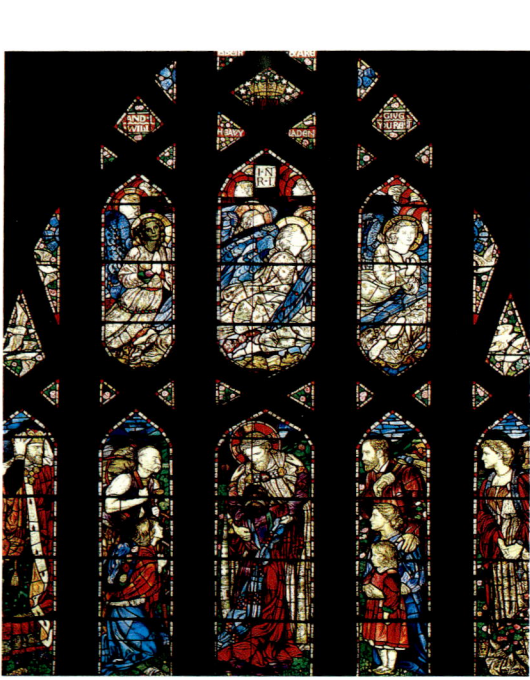

Above Chancel with panelling by Gimson. The 'door' to the ventilation shaft can be seen beside the altar.
Above left Altar hanging made in the Morris & Co workshops after a design by Burne-Jones.
Left Lady Chapel stained-glass window by A H Payne. Taking as its text 'Come unto me all who are heavy laden and I will give you rest', it celebrates the dignity of labour as represented by local trades and individuals. Apparently the 'black angel' is a result of trial firing of the glass.

Right The chancel ceiling was painted 20 years after the church had been consecrated. Prior's design took Creation as its theme, the allusion to origins chiming nicely with the stone tracery suggesting a Gothic architecture having its origins in the rudimentary 'megalithic' masonry of Saxon Britain when our first churches were built.

Above and right Details of oak choir stalls by Gimson and Barnsley. Their furniture at this time made extensive and elaborate use of chamfering. Derived from the wheelwright's craft this 'decoration' brought the message of the craftsman's contribution to design directly to the congregation.
Far right The Lady Chapel.

41

Prior's patented 'Early English Glass' was used throughout and makes an extraordinary contribution to the space of the church. The unevenness of thickness and irregularities encouraged in the process of making gives a subtle variation to the light as it plays across the deep stone reveals.

The coupled columns support the springing of the stone arches and allow passage along the sides of the nave. They were inspired by similar columns at the nearby Saxon church of St Peter, Monkwearmouth. The simple cushion capitals are like the first Romanesque capitals that masons developed in response to their invention of the arch.
Above Font carved from Marsden stone by A Randall Wells, the site architect.

Crosses and candlesticks by Gimson and Barnsley's blacksmith Alfred Bucknall. Beaten from wrought iron they are lacquered to prevent rusting. The ebony lectern with inlaid mother-of-pearl and silver was designed and made by Ernest Gimson.

Location plan

Drawings

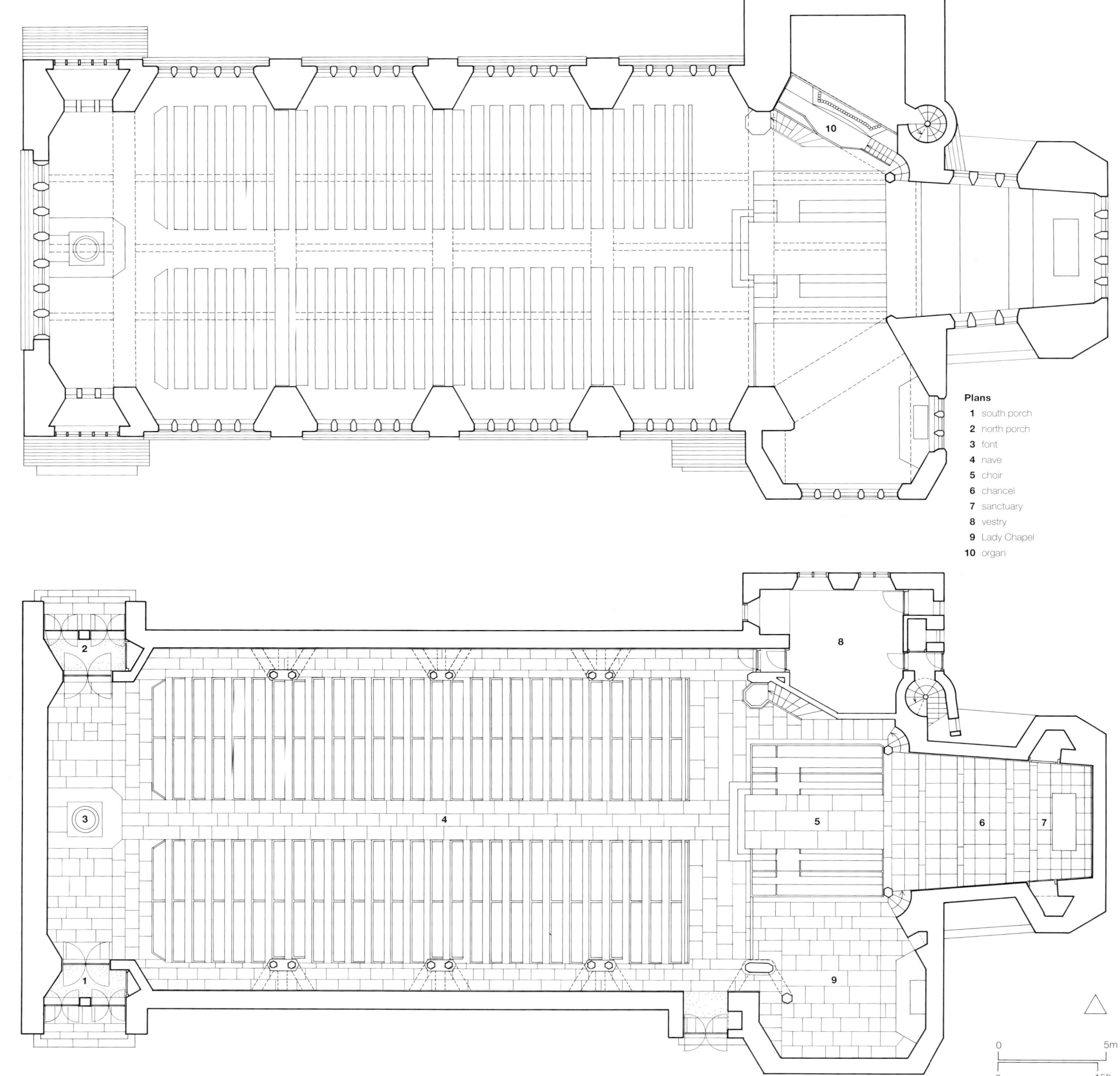

Plans
1 south porch
2 north porch
3 font
4 nave
5 choir
6 chancel
7 sanctuary
8 vestry
9 Lady Chapel
10 organ

Cross section facing east

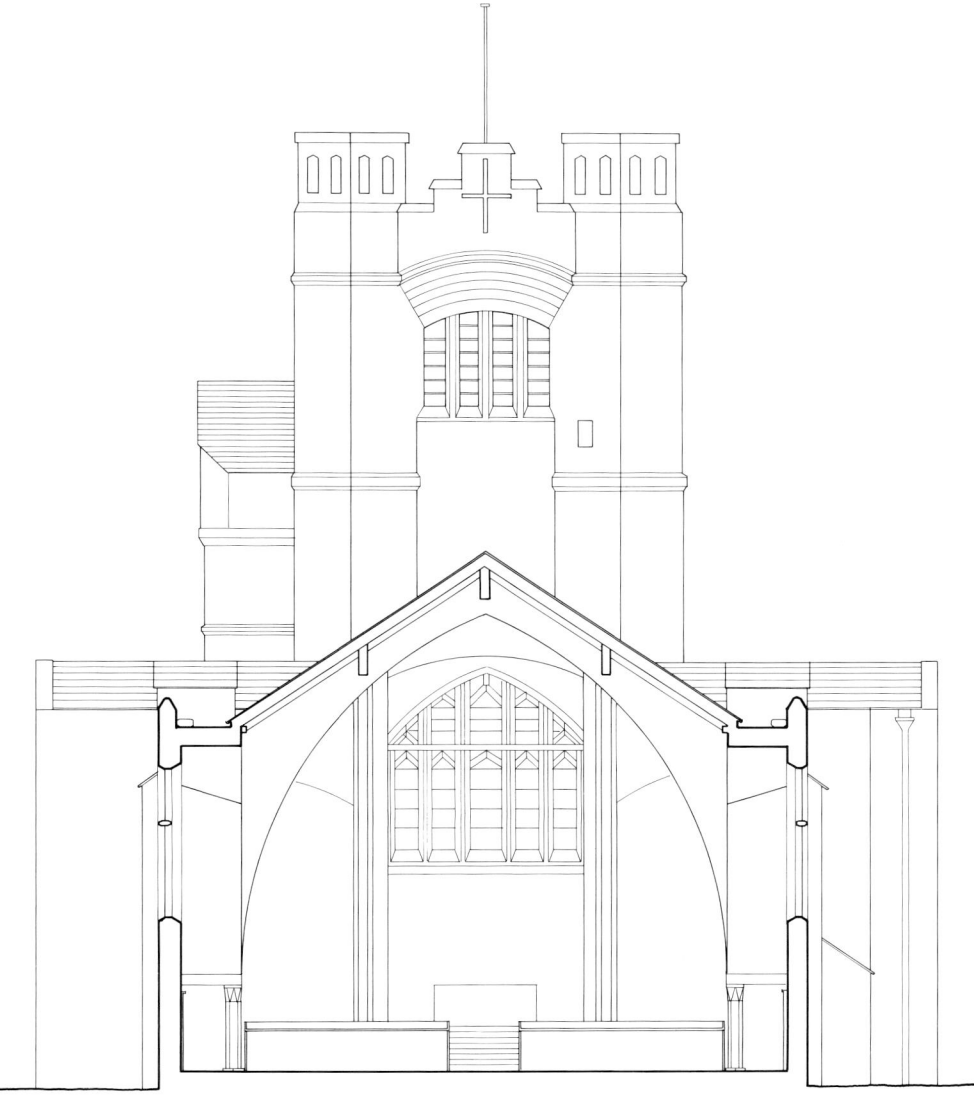

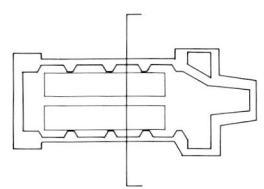

Long elevation facing south

50

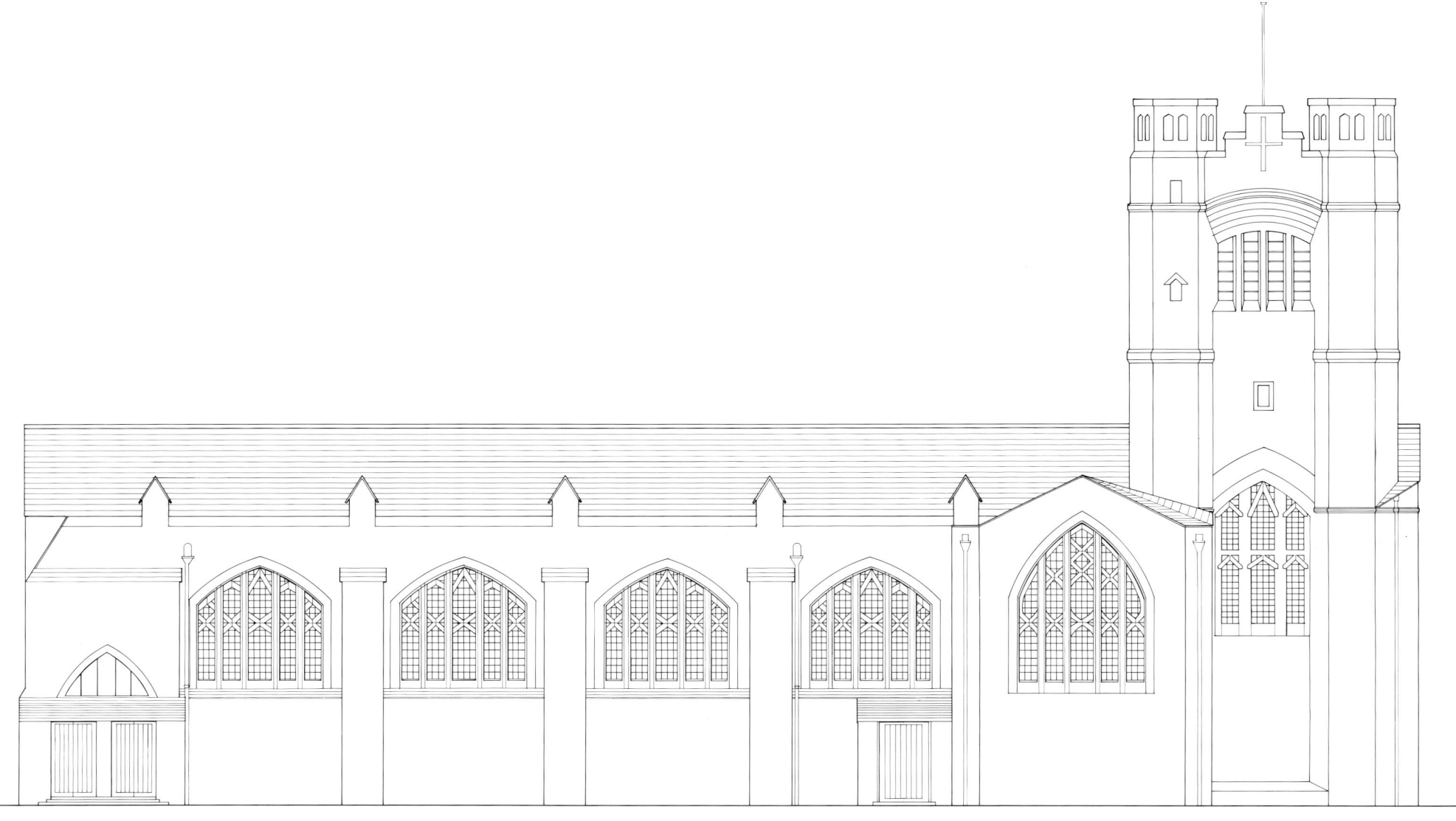

End elevations

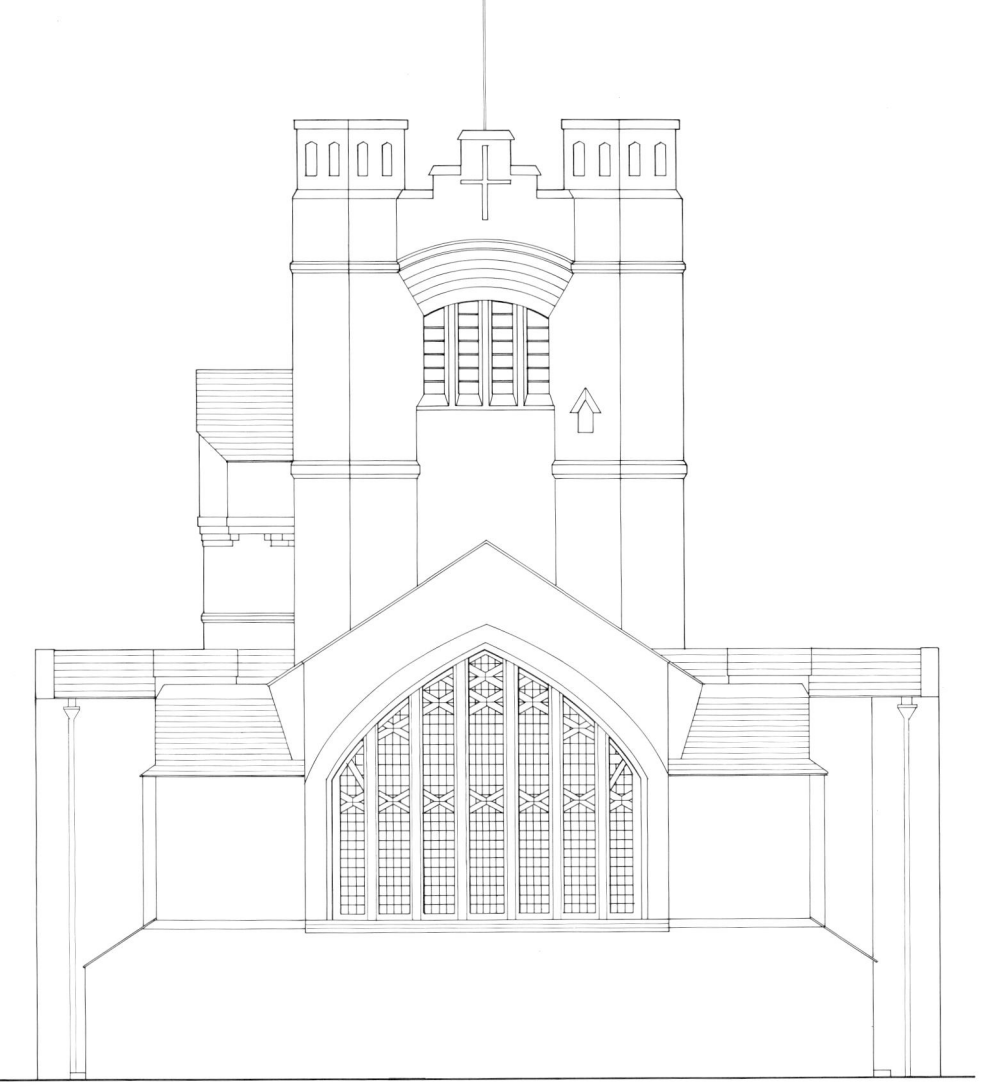

West elevation

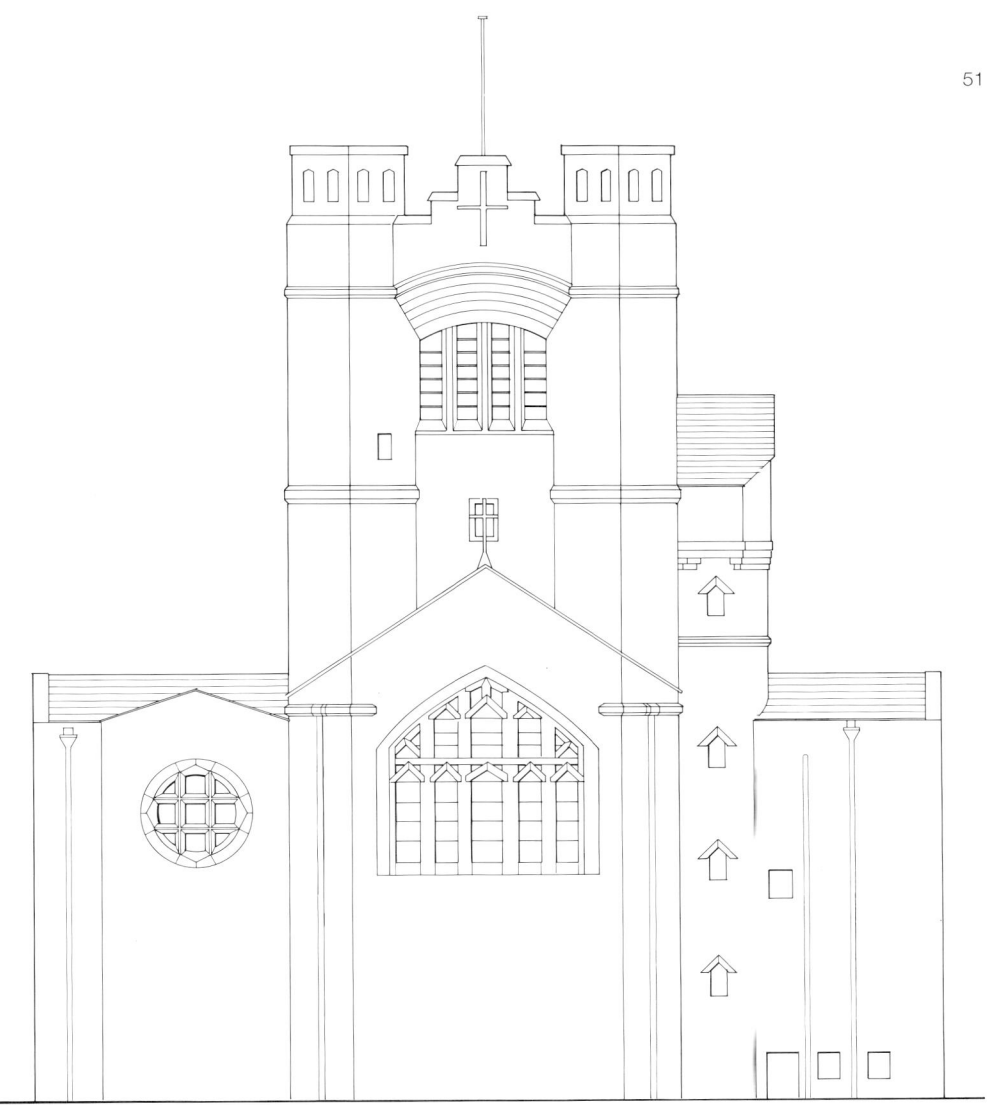

East elevation

Plan and elevation of typical nave bay

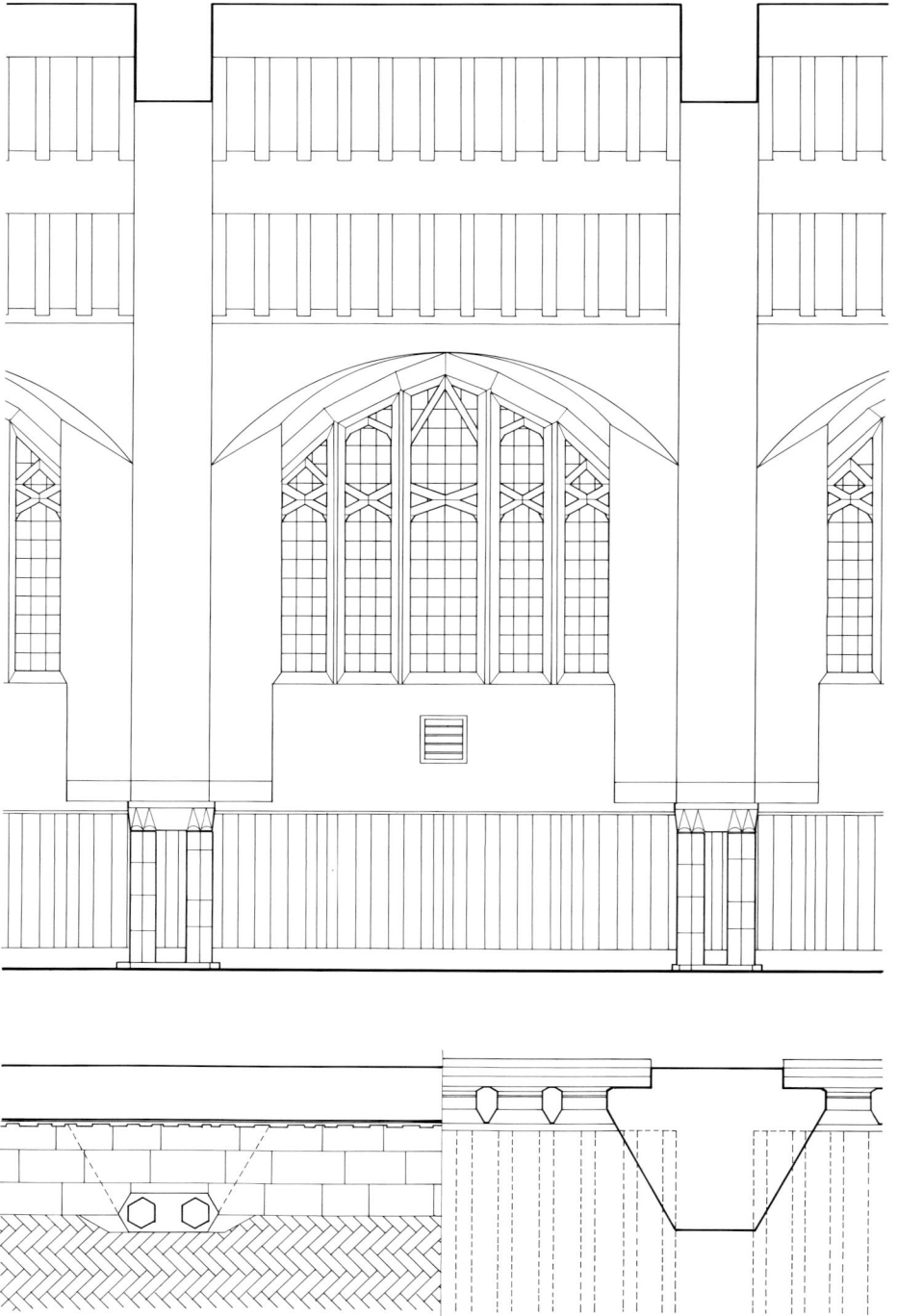
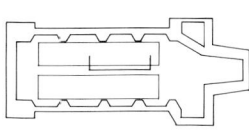

Part section through nave and column details

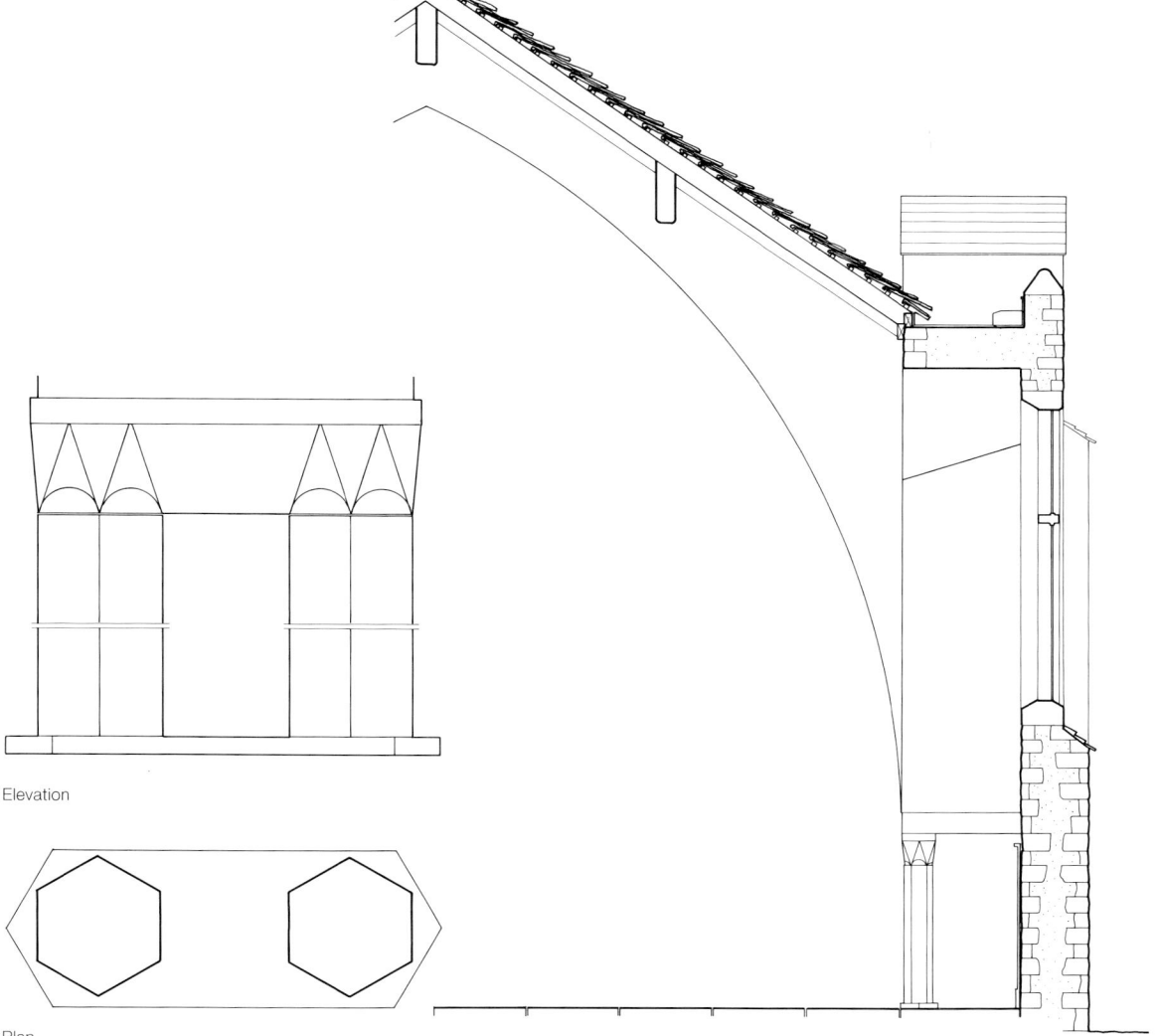

Elevation

Plan

Column details

Section through nave facing east

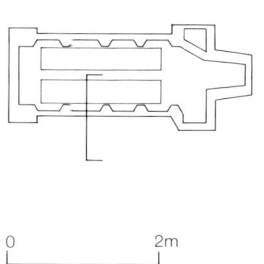

Plan and elevation of chancel

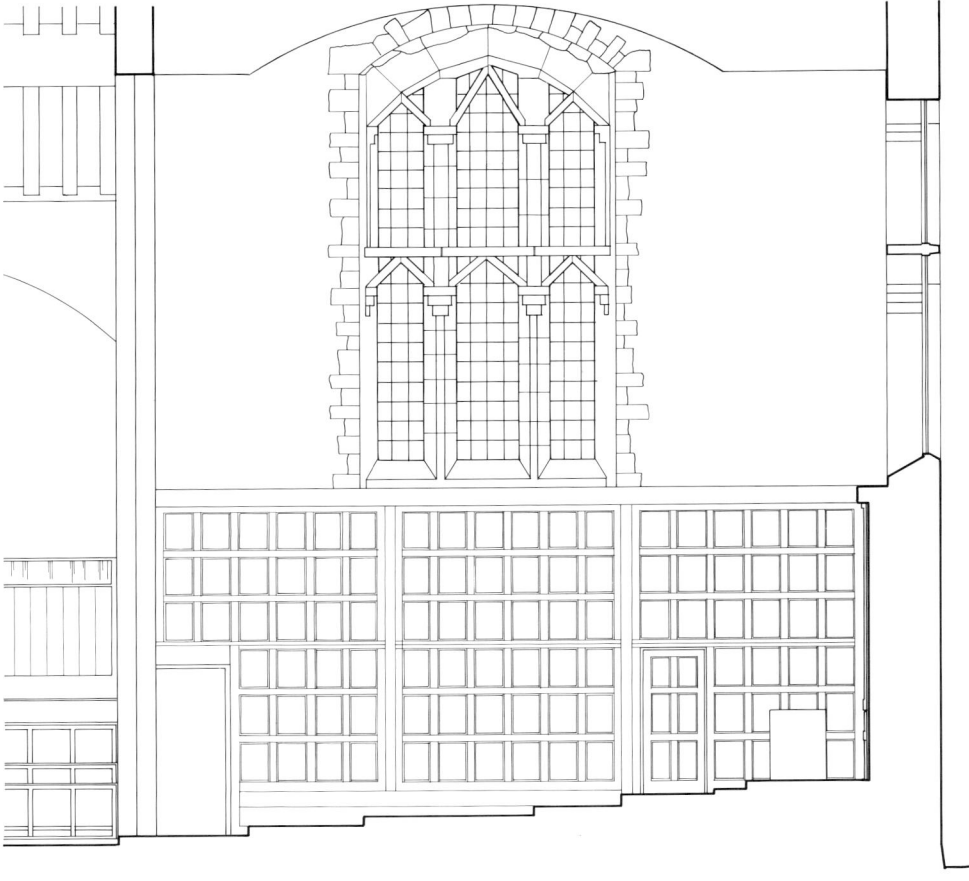

Elevation of chancel

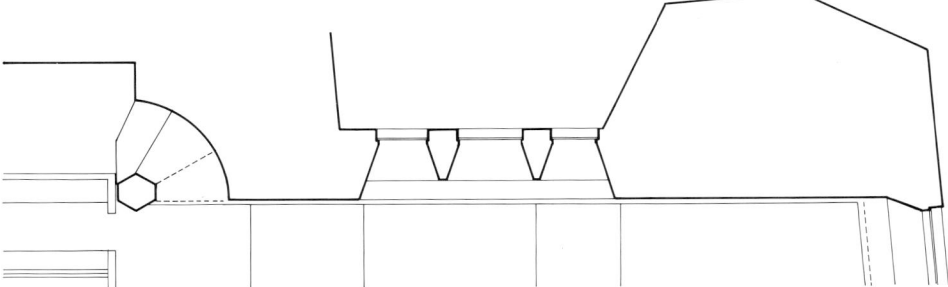

Plan of chancel

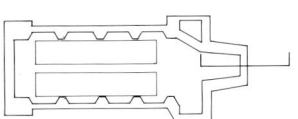

Detail of choir stalls

Elevation to typical bay

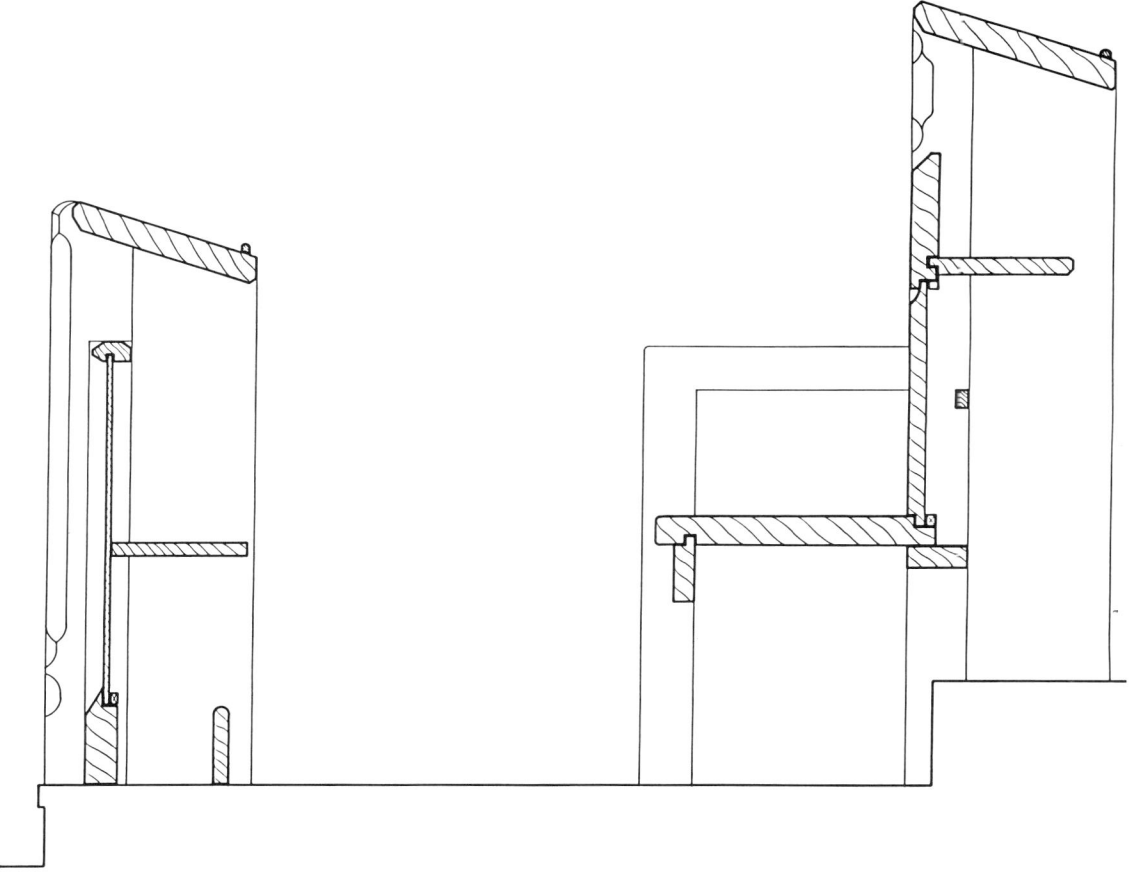

Cross section through choir stalls

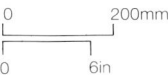

Section and elevation to south entrance

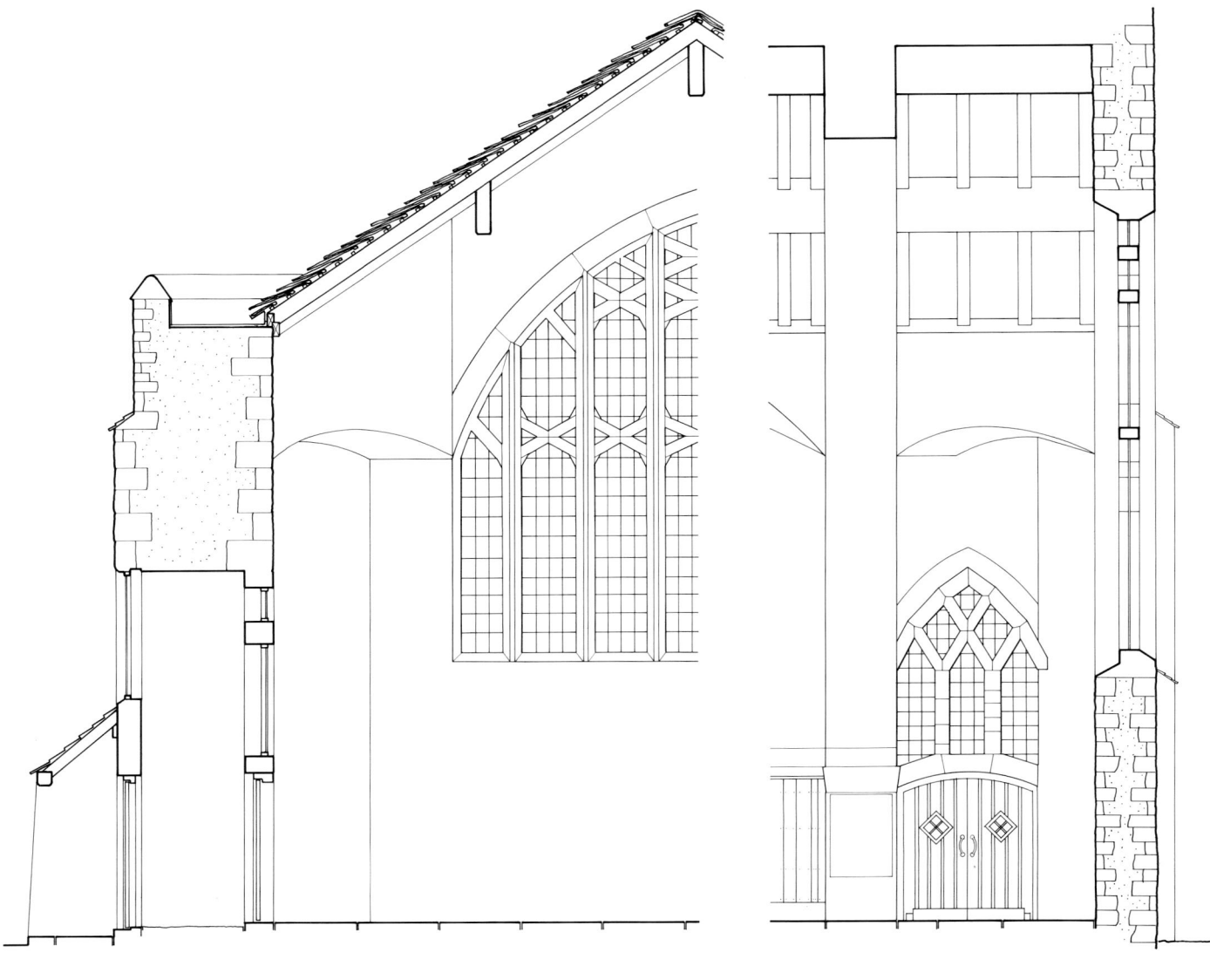

Section through south entrance

Internal elevation to south entrance

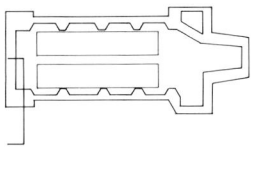

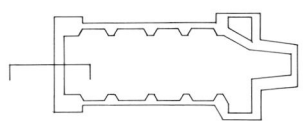

Internal elevation to south entrance doors

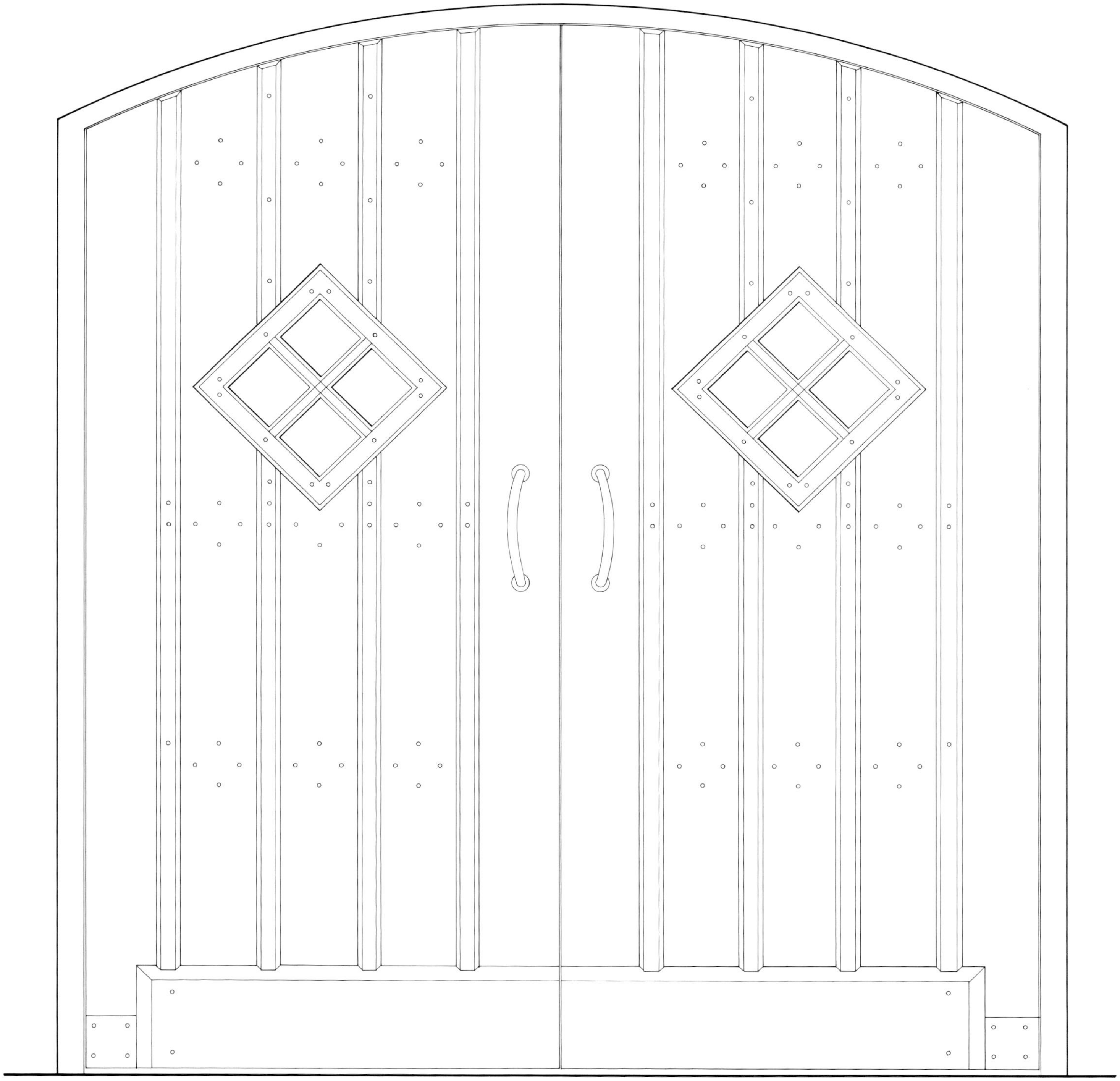

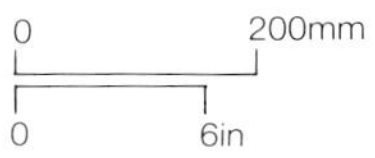

57

0 200mm
0 6in

Author's acknowledgements

I would like to thank the Reverend Michael Berk and Mark Worthington the Curate of St Andrew's for the assistance and courtesy extended on my several visits to the church. Thanks also to the staff of the Durham County Records Office and the RIBA Drawings Collection who helped with the research. I am particularly grateful to Martin Charles, not only for the photographs, but for some provocative insights that aided the enquiry. Kingston University supported the research by assisting with travel costs. Finally thanks to Margy for patiently typing the several drafts.

Illustration acknowledgements

Black and white referential illustrations have been provided courtesy of the following: British Architectural Library, RIBA, London: figs 3, 9, 10, 26, 29, 39, and back cover; Martin Charles: figs 1, 15, 16, 23, 24, 30, 32, 38, 40, 41, 43–51; © Country Life Picture Library: fig 33; RCHME © Crown Copyright: figs 35–37.

Chronology

1852 Edward Schroeder Prior born 4 June.

1855 Father dies in a riding accident.

1856 Mother moves the family to Harrow where Prior will attend school.

1870 Enters Gonville and Caius College, Cambridge.

1872 Represents Cambridge in High Jump, Long Jump and Hurdles against Oxford, and wins the British Amateur High Jump.

1874 Articled to Norman Shaw.

1877 Begins his stint as Clerk of Works on Shaw's St Margaret's, Ilkley. Study tour of Belgium with Ernest Newton. Morris & Co opens showroom in Oxford Street. Morris gives his first public lecture on 'The Decorative Arts'.

1879 Begins his own practice with a setting-up commission from Shaw of Carr Manor, near Leeds. A series of buildings in and around Harrow and Bridport formed the basis of his practice.

1882 Morris's first collection of essays 'Hope and Fears for Art' published.

1884 Founding member of the Art Workers' Guild. 11 August marries Louise Isabella, second daughter of the Rev F W Maunsell of Symondsbury, Dorset. The couple were to have two daughters. Prior designed with William Lethaby a memorial window for St John the Baptist Church where he was married. Commission for Holy Trinity, Bothenhampton, Quay Terrace, Bridport.

1885 Design for Henry Martyn Hall, Cambridge.

1887 Elected Fellow of the RIBA, proposed by E J May, J Belcher and A Blomfield.

1888 First Arts and Crafts Exhibition Societies public show.

1889 Delivers his first public lecture entitled 'Texture as a Condition of Art and a Necessity for Architecture' to the Edinburgh Congress of National Association for the Advancement of Art in Relation to Industry. Morris was in the Chair. Begins to produce 'Prior's Early English Glass'.

1890 Designs the Harrow Music School building.

1891 Designs Pembroke College Mission in Walworth. Architects' Registration Bill put before Parliament.

1892 Prior contributes an article entitled 'The Profession and its Ghosts' to the collection 'Architecture: a Profession or an Art?' edited by Shaw and T G Jackson. He resigns from the RIBA in protest against its examination policy.

1894 Moves to 10 Melina Place, St John's Wood. Voysey lives next door and probably influences his design for the swimming baths at Bridport.

1895 Exhibits wax model of a radical house at the Royal Academy.

1896 Design for The Barn, Exmouth. He lives close by for long periods to supervise the construction. Morris dies.

1900 His first book, 'The History of Gothic Art in England', is published.

1901 He is appointed to the editorial board of the *Architectural Review*. He contributes a series of articles thereafter.

1902 Secretary of the Arts and Crafts Exhibitions Society.

1903 Design for Kelling Place (later Home Place), Holt, Norfolk. A Randall Wells acts as site architect. Roker and Fulwell New Church Committee formed in October. John Priestman, a local shipbuilder, donates £6,000 towards the new church.

1904 Design for Medical Schools, Cambridge. The Bishop of Durham consents to the division of the parish of Monkwearmouth and Prior gives estimate of £9,980 to build St Andrew's.

1905 Priestman chairs a new informal committee to oversee the final stages of design. Prior's estimate set of drawings are dated May.

1906 Randall Wells sets out St Andrew's in January and remains living close by to supervise work throughout. Ecclesiastical Commissioners approve the church but with reservations concerning the unusual column arrangements. Foundation stone laid by Mrs Priestman on 12 June. Prior is Master of the Art Workers' Guild.

1907 Randall Wells's reply to the Commissioners concerns in January suggest that walls are constructed. The church is consecrated on 19 July. The total cost of the church is £13,117, the fabric costing £7,881-8-4, furnishings £5,255-11-8.

1912 Appointed Slade Professor of Architectural History at Cambridge. Publishes 'An Account of Medieval Figure Sculpture in England'.

1913 Designs St Edmund's Church, Parkstone, Dorset, with Arthur Grove.

1922 Publishes 'Eight Chapters on English Medieval Art'.

1927 Produces design for the chancel of St Andrew's, executed by MacDonald Gill.

1932 Prior dies on 19 August. He was buried in an unmarked grave at St Mary's, Apuldram.

Select Bibliography

Addleshaw G and F Etchells, *The Architectural Setting of Anglican Worship* (Faber & Faber: London, 1948). Subtitled 'An Inquiry into the arrangements for Public Worship in the Church of England from the Reformation to the present day', this is a good survey resulting from the collaboration of canon and architect.

Comito M, *Gimson and the Barnsleys* (Evan Bros Ltd: London, 1980). This is the only book-length treatment of these important furniture designers and architects who took Morris's call to the crafts most to heart.

Davey P, *Arts and Crafts Architecture* (Phaidon: London, 1994). A well illustrated, extensive and witty survey of the work of all its leading proponents.

Goodhart-Rendell H, *English Architecture since the Regency* (Constable & Co: London, 1953). First delivered as the Slade Lectures, this remains one of the best general guides to Victorian Architecture, delivered with the passion of a late participant.

Hoare G, and G Pyne, *Prior's Barn and Gimson's Coxen; Two Arts & Crafts Houses* (privately published from 'Selforth', Little Knowle, Budleigh Salterton, 1978). A detailed account of Prior's first radical building, drawing upon the knowledge of local historians.

Lambourne L, *Utopian Craftsmen* (Astragal Books: London, 1980). Although Prior is only mentioned in passing this book is one of the best general surveys of the Arts and Crafts movement well capturing its spirit and philosophy.

Lethaby W, *Philip Webb and his Work* (Raven Oak Press: London, 1979). This is probably the best book of Lethaby's many to understand the architectural source of Prior's inspiration, in particular the chapter entitled 'Some architects of the 19th Century and Two Ways of building'.

Massé H, *The Art Workers' Guild, 1884–1934* (Shakespeare Head Press: Oxford, 1935). This definitive account of the Guild which became the principal forum of the Arts and Crafts movement, includes a chapter on its origins written by Prior.

Morris W, *Architecture, Industry and Wealth* (Longmans, Green & Co: London, 1902). This collection of his essays is to be recommended for its concentration upon architecture.

Pevsner N, *Some Architectural Writers of the Nineteenth Century*, (Clarendon Press: Oxford, 1972). Good accounts of all the noteworthy writers provide an essential picture of the background to Prior's thinking about architecture. Kerr's essay 'English Architecture Thirty Years Hence' and Morris's 'The Revival of Architecture' are reprinted as Appendices.

Prior E S, *The Cathedral Builders of England* (Seeley & Co: London, 1905).

Prior E S, *Eight Chapters on English Medieval Architecture*, (Cambridge University Press, 1922).

Prior E S, *A History of Gothic Art in England* (George Bell and Sons: London, 1900).

Prior E S, *Medieval Figure Sculpture in England* (Cambridge University Press, 1912). All four of Prior's books, as the titles indicate, dealt with his favourite architecture from slightly different viewpoints. Like his friend Lethaby, he dug into the Cathedral building rolls to glean information on medieval masons to supplement his vast first-hand experience of the buildings.

Ruskin J, *Lectures on Art and Architecture* (George Routledge & Son: London, 1854). The Edinburgh Lectures make a good introduction to Ruskin's thoughts on architecture for he presented them as a summary of his earlier *Seven Lamps of Architecture* and *The Stones of Venice*.

Saint A, *Richard Norman Shaw* (Yale University Press: New Haven and London, 1976). The definitive and a model biography of this great Victorian architect includes a good chapter on the office as it was when Prior was a pupil of Shaw.

Service A, *Edwardian Architecture* (Thames and Hudson: London, 1977). A successful summary of the material collected in a book of essays he edited earlier, *Edwardian Architecture and its Origins* (Architectural Press: London, 1975) which includes a short pioneering study of Prior's work by Christopher Grillet.

Summerson J, *The Turn of the Century; Architecture in Britain around 1900* (University of Glasgow Press, 1976). Originally delivered as the W A Cagill Memorial Lecture, this makes a good introduction to the period, for it sketches a picture of the events, mood and all the important architects working around 1900 delivered with the author's inimitable wit and breadth.

Notes

1. *St Andrew's Vestry Records Book*. Annual Parochial Church Meeting, 22 April 1927, Durham County Archives, EP/Mo SA 6/1.
2. E S Prior, 'The New Cathedral for Liverpool', *Architectural Review*, 1901 (vol 10), p144.
3. N Pevsner, *The Buildings of England; Northumberland* (Penguin Books: London, 1953), p469.
4. Some biographical information on Prior can be found in the RIBA Library but the details here are drawn from the unpublished PhD of Lynne Walker, *E S Prior 1852–1932*, Birkbeck College, University of London, 1978.
5. A Saint, *Richard Norman Shaw* (Yale University Press: New Haven and London, 1976), p130. See pp185–91 for details of Shaw's pupils and assistants.
6. Walker, *op cit*, pp81–2.
7. Saint, *op cit*, pp295 and 417.
8. H Goodhart-Rendell, 'Rogue Architects of the Victorian Age', *RIBA Journal*, April 1949 (vol 56), p257.
9. Saint, *op cit*, p186. This comment was ascribed to Shaw by his son Robert Shaw in manuscript notes on his father.
10. Obituaries appeared in *The Architect*, 26 August 1932, p236, *RIBA Journal*, 15 October 1932, pp858–9, and *The Builder*, 26 August 1932, p328.
11. Walker, *op cit*, p104. Prior's client was Thomas Allbutt, an enlightened medical practitioner whom George Eliot used as model for Tertius Lydgate in *Middlemarch*.
12. Saint, *op cit*, p406.
13. Walker, *op cit*, pp313–49. Holy Trinity was largely paid for by J Gundy, Chairman of the West Bay Building Company.
14. H Massé, *The Art Workers' Guild, 1884–1934* (Shakespeare Head Press: Oxford, 1935), p7.
15. *ibid*.
16. R Kerr, 'English Architecture Thirty Years Hence' in N Pevsner, *Some Architectural Thinkers of the 19th Century* (Clarendon Press: Oxford, 1972), pp309–10.
17. J Ruskin, *Lectures on Arts and Architecture* (George Routledge & Son: London, 1854), p111.
18. E S Prior, *The Origins of the Guild*, in Massé, *op cit*, p8.
19. *Ibid*, p11.
20. *Ibid*, p12.
21. May Morris, *The Introductions to the Collected Works of William Morris*, vol 2 (Oriole Editions: New York, 1973), p460. The Arts and Crafts Exhibition Society was formed to publicize the work of AWG members which its own constitution forbade. Morris was on the selection committee for the first show. He proposed the formation of the NAAA in September 1888. E Lemire, *The Unpublished Lectures of William Morris* (Wayne State University Press: Detroit, 1969), p272.
22. Lemire, *op cit*, p280; and *Transactions of the National Association for the Advancement of Art*, 1890, p332. In the discussion that followed Prior's paper he disagreed with Morris's contention that there could never be an iron architecture.
23. E S Prior, 'Texture as a Quality of Art and a Condition for Architecture', *Transactions, op cit*, p319.
24. *Ibid*, pp319–21.
25. *Ibid*, p320.
26. *Ibid*, pp322–3.
27. *Ibid*, p322.
28. W Morris, 'The Revival of Architecture' in *Architecture, Industry and Wealth* (Longmans, Green & Co: London, 1902), p198.
29. Wordsworth and Coleridge, *The Lyrical Ballads*, eds R Brett and A Jones, (Methuen & Co Ltd: London, 1963), pp261 and 244.
30. S T Coleridge, *Biographia Literaria* (Dent & Son: London, 1965), p167.
31. W Morris, 'The Influence of Building Materials upon Architecture' in *Architecture, Industry and Wealth, op cit*, p250.
32. See T Garnham, *The Oxford Museum* (Phaidon: London, 1992), for a discussion of this.
33. Prior, *op cit*, p322.
34. *Ibid*.
35. *Ibid*.

36 Jacquetta Hawkes in her book *A Land* (The Cresset Press: London, 1951), explores the conundrum of where one draws the line between us and nature, given the theory of evolution; the monkey, the mollusc, microbes, or the rocks laid down from primeval mud?
37 Prior, *op cit*, p322.
38 *Ibid*, p329.
39 E S Prior, 'Architectural Modelling' in *The Builder*, 29 June 1895 (vol 68) p483.
40 *Ibid*. Up to Soane's time models were commonly used, but Prior's was only the second model at the RA in 20 years
41 The client for The Barn, W H Weatherhall, was an old Harrovian. G Hoare and G Pyne, *Prior's Barn and Gimson's Coxen; Two Arts and Crafts Houses* (privately published with unnumbered pages).
42 Prior read Viollet-le-Duc's *Discourse* published in 1889 in which he illustrates an X-plan town house.
43 Prior was a keen butterfly collector.
44 *Architectural Review*, 1906 (vol 19) p70.
45 H M Taylor and Joan Taylor, *Anglo-Saxon Architecture* (Cambridge University Press, 1965), p338. Bishop Biscop brought John the archchanter to teach the Gregorian chant which was first sung in these islands at St Peter's. Bede also had an association with this monastic settlement.
46 St Peter's, Monkwearmouth is mentioned for its western porch in Prior's *A History of Gothic Art in England* (George Bell & Sons, London, 1900), p48.
47 Copy Letter book relating to the building of the new church, 19 October 1903. Durham County Records. EP/Mo SA/1.
48 *Ibid*. Letter to S O Austen, 30 December 1903.
49 Priestman & Co, established in 1882, was a typical late nineteenth-century shipyard that grew from little more than a one-man workshop to become a large, industrial concern. This was the dawn of iron steamers, Priestman & Co specializing in the design and construction of tramp steamers. It is estimated that he donated more than £½ million to charitable concerns during his lifetime and he left £1,504,744 at his death. He received a knighthood in 1913 and a Baronetcy in 1934 in recognition of his public works.
50 Letter from Chairman of the Roker and Fulwell New Church Committee to Priestman, 20 April 1904. Durham County Archives, EP/Mo SA/1.
51 Charles Prior was son-in-law of BF Westcott, the previous Bishop who had died in 1901. He was also a close friend of the vicar of All Saints, Monkwearmouth, the Rev D S Bontflower, a former student of Caius. Walker, *op cit*, p473.
52 This information is given in a summary of events pertaining to the commission and building of St Andrew's, drawn up as a result of a dispute between Priestman and church wardens. It seems that Priestman lent £1,206 in 1909 and that the church wardens were unable or reluctant to repay. In January 1910 Priestman wrote to the Chairman that he 'never though [he] would behave in such a contemptible way'. Durham County Archives EP/Mo SA4/3.
53 Lethaby had introduced a 'School of Handicraft and Design' to the Architectural Association where he prompted his radical views. In a talk to the School Prior said: '… that he belonged to the same school of architectural thought as Mr Lethaby, … the school which believed that architecture was rational building'. *AA Notes*, November 1896, Vol II, p120. See T Garnham, 'William Lethaby and the Two Ways of Building', *AA Files*, No 10, Autumn 1985, pp27–43 for discussion of this.
54 E S Prior, 'Church building as it is and how it might be', *Architectural Review*, 1898, p157.
55 E S Prior, *The New Cathedral for Liverpool, op cit*, pp145–6.
56 J Davies (ed), *A New Dictionary of Liturgy and Worship* (SCM Press Ltd: London, 1986), p 3. See also G Addleshaw & and F Etchells, *The Architectural Setting of Anglican Worship*, (Faber & Fabe: London, 1948).
57 E S Prior, 'Art Study at Cambridge', *RIBA Journal*, 29 June 1912, p594.
58 Rev D Marsh, *Description and Notes concerning the Church of St Andrew's, Roker*, p27. Prior described Fulwell as 'A quarry of beautiful limestone … [but] the craft of using it in building had died out.' *The Builder*, 12 October 1907 (vol 93) p386.
59 A Randall Wells, Letter to the Ecclesiastical Commissioners, 3 January 1907. Durham County Archives EP/Mo SA 4/56 (1).
60 Letter from Ecclesiastical Commissioners, 21 February 1906, Durham County Archives EP/Mo SA/55(1).
61 Prior, *A History of Gothic Art in England, op cit*, pp46–9.
62 W R Lethaby, *The Church of Sancta Sophia* (Macmillan & Co: London, 1894), p247.
63 Randall Wells, *op cit*.
64 Randall Wells, *The Builder*, 7 November 1907 (vol 93) p563.
65 Marsh, *op cit*, pp17–18.
66 RIBA Drawings Collection, RAN 5/H/4 1–15.
67 Ironically Shaw was on the panel that rejected Prior's design on 1 December 1886. In November a panel containing J D Sedding and James Brook said that: 'The character of the roofing proposed is extraordinary, expensive and unsafe, and not to be recommended according to construction and decor, though the idea is a suggestive one.' Walker, *op cit*, pp330–31.
68 Prior, letter to *The Builder*, 23 November 1907, pp562–3.
69 Wells, *op cit*.
70 The Congress was extensively reported in the Journal of the RIBA, 25 August 1906 (vol XIII). Otto Wagner attended. Prior was Master of the AWG in this year and chaired a conference on William Morris held to coincide with the Congress. See Massé, *op cit*, pp113–14.
71 Prior described the Gothic of the Ile de France as 'Chairworks of articulated stone pegged to the ground by pinnacles', *A History of Gothic Art, op cit*, p9. But he disagreed with Lethaby's view that all European Gothic was in some way the offspring of this 'Mother' art.
72 Prior, *Eight Chapters on Medieval Art* (Cambridge University Press, 1922), p1.
73 Taylor and Taylor, *op cit*.
74 Prior, *The New Cathedral for Liverpool*, p143.
75 Prior, *Eight Chapters on English Medieval Art, op cit*, p9.
76 Prior had worked on restorations at Kelsale and Framlingham in Suffolk. He mentions Blythburgh, a particularly fine example of this type in his *Cathedral Builders of England*, (Seeley & Co: London, 1905), p94.
77 Marsh, *op cit*, p2.
78 Saint, *op cit*, pp276–93.
79 Prior, *Eight Chapters on English Medieval Art, op cit*, p131.
80 Prior, *A History of Gothic Art in England, op cit*, pp428 and 447–8.
81 Semper was in England helping to prepare the Great Exhibition. There is a manuscript – 'Practical Art in Metals, its Technology, History and Styles' – at the Victoria and Albert Museum (MS 86 ff 64) where his early thoughts that lead to his monumental *Der Stil* could have been read by Prior's circle.
82 Gimson had met Morris when he was only 19 and had been given an introduction to the office of J D Sedding by him. M Comito, *Gimson and the Barnsleys* (Evans Bros Ltd: London, 1980), pp13–15. The following account is drawn from this book; see in particular pp102–6.
83 This account of the church furnishing draws extensively upon the Rev Marsh's description.
84 Marsh, *op cit*, p15.
85 *Ibid*, p11.
86 Prior's specification cited in Walker, *op cit*, p384. This technique would produce glass only up to 8 x 6 in. Christopher Whall used Prior's glass.
87 Marsh, *op cit*, p18.
88 *Ibid*.
89 *Ibid*, p29.
90 *Ibid*, p11.
91 *Ibid*.